INTRODUCTION

Aerobatic display teams – brightly-coloured aircraft flown in formation by some of the world's most skilled pilots – are one of the wonders of the modern world.

Every year airshow goers in their hundreds of thousands are able to marvel at the breath-taking spectacle that is an aerobatic flying demonstration. With expert pilots at the controls, flights of light and nimble aircraft can be made to appear as though they are dancing on air, swooping, looping, wingtip to wingtip, tumbling, dashing, trailing smoke to create remarkable patterns in the sky.

And they are fantastically rare. Flying complex manoeuvres requires a level of concentration, dedication, training and courage that very few possess, so the number of pilots able to participate in formation aerobatics is incredibly small. The more ambitious the routines and manoeuvres, and the larger the formation, the more skilled the display pilots need to be.

Then there are the aircraft. Maintaining a fleet of complex aircraft for the sake of aerobatic flying requires fuel for both performances and training, not to mention spare parts and consumables as well as dedicated engineers and maintenance personnel who can be spared from the main air force for such duties.

Only the most well-funded air forces can afford their own team. So why, then, do those countries that have one (or more) continue to support aerobatic display flying? What makes them so special, beyond their sheer rarity? For the air force, a display team is an obvious means of showcasing the raw talent, enviable skill and outstanding training of its pilots. In some cases, it is a point of pride too that the aircraft flown are locally made – their manoeuvrability, reliability and sometimes special abilities being shown off both at home and often abroad too.

A display team can also prove to be a powerful recruiting tool. Potential new air force personnel might see the team and decide that they would like to try flying for themselves one day.

For audiences, the appeal of seeing an aerobatic team in action is clear – the dazzling sight of aircraft, fast or slow, being flown together in unison, leaving smoke trails, flying tricky manoeuvres, making low passes, turning in the air together just feet apart, or even performing unusual tricks, can be truly awe-inspiring.

Beyond all that, modern aerobatic teams embody the sheer joy and thrill of flight. Since the earliest days of aviation, pilots have attempted to fly aircraft together in formation – to demonstrate their own mastery of the air – and modern teams continue that proud tradition.

A key component of any aerobatic team is the colours worn by its aircraft. Many feature a patriotic scheme derived from their national flag, while others bear historic colours or simply bright patterns intended to help the aircraft stand out against the sky.

This publication chronicles the schemes worn by aerobatic team aircraft from the 1950s right up to the present day through the beautiful artworks of renowned aviation illustrator JP Vieira. I hope you enjoy marvelling at the incredible variety of designs as much as I have.

Dan Sharp

ABOUT THE ARTIST

JP Vieira is an illustrator producing military history and aviation-themed artwork.

He is entirely self-taught and aims to constantly improve both his technical and digital methods. His attention to detail and constant pursuit of improvement makes his artworks both accurate and artistically pleasing.

JP has collaborated with numerous authors, editors and publishers on a wide variety of publications – including USAF Fighters, US Navy Jet Fighters, Marine Corps Jet Fighters, US Jet Fighters in Foreign Service, French Combat Jets and most recently Air National Guard Jet Fighters for Tempest Books.

The US Air Force's Air Demonstration Squadron, the Thunderbirds, perform at Hill Air Force Base, Utah, on June 28, 2024. The Thunderbirds are a team of roughly 130 personnel that demonstrate the pride, precision and professionalism of the total US Air Force. (USAF photo by Staff Sergeant Dakota Carter)

MODERN AEROBATIC TEAMS

Contents

CHAPTER 1 – EUROPE

Austria	006
Belgium	008
Belarus	010
Croatia	010
Czech Republic	012
Denmark	012
Finland	012
France	014
Germany	018
Greece	020
Hungary	020
Ireland	022
Italy	024
Netherlands	028
Norway	030
Poland	030
Portugal	032
Russia	036
Slovakia	038
Spain	038
Sweden	040
Switzerland	042
Turkey	044
United Kingdom	048
Yugoslavia	058
Ukraine	058

CHAPTER 2 – NORTH AMERICA

Canada	060
USA	066

CHAPTER 3 – SOUTH/CENTRAL AMERICA

Argentina	082
Brazil	084

Chile	086
El Salvador	088
Mexico	088
Peru	090
Venezuela	090

CHAPTER 4 – AFRICA

Egypt	092
Morocco	092
South Africa	094

CHAPTER 5 – ASIA

Brunei	096
China	096
India	100
Indonesia	104
Iran	108
Israel	110
Japan	112
Jordan	114
Malaysia	114
Pakistan	116
Philippines	118
Saudi Arabia	120
Singapore	120
South Korea	122
Taiwan	124
Thailand	124
United Arab Emirates	124

CHAPTER 6 – OCEANIA

Australia	126
New Zealand	128

All illustrations:
JP VIEIRA

Design:
DRUCK MEDIA PVT. LTD.

Publisher:
STEVE O'HARA

Production editor:
DAN SHARP

Published by:
MORTONS MEDIA GROUP LTD, MEDIA CENTRE, MORTON WAY, HORNCASTLE, LINCOLNSHIRE LN9 6JR.

Tel. 01507 529529

ISBN: 978-1-911703-46-4

© 2024 MORTONS MEDIA GROUP LTD. ALL RIGHTS RESERVED. NO PART OF THIS PUBLICATION MAY BE REPRODUCED OR TRANSMITTED IN ANY FORM OR BY ANY MEANS, ELECTRONIC OR MECHANICAL, INCLUDING PHOTOCOPYING, RECORDING, OR ANY INFORMATION STORAGE RETRIEVAL SYSTEM WITHOUT PRIOR PERMISSION IN WRITING FROM THE PUBLISHER.

MODERN AEROBATIC TEAMS — CHAPTER 1 — EUROPE

CHAPTER 1 – EUROPE

AUSTRIA

▼ FOUGA CM 170 MAGISTER

Fouga CM 170 Magister, 4D-YK/358, Silver Birds, Österreichische Luftstreitkräfte (Austrian Air Force), Zeltweg Airbase, Austria, 1967.
Having being formed to fly the Fouga Magister, the Silver Birds did so from 1966 until 1968; they briefly re-formed in 1975 with the Saab 105, but were disbanded a year later.

SILVER BIRDS, AUSTRIAN AIR FORCE

Austria bought 18 Fouga CM 170R Magister two-seat jet trainers from France in 1959 and seven years later they became the mounts of the Austrian Air Force's first aerobatic team – the Silver Birds. The team operated a quartet of Magisters for two years prior to being disbanded in 1968. The Magisters were retired four years after that but by then Austria had become the sole export customer for the Saab 105 under the designation 105Ö. This improved version was intended not only as a trainer but also for reconnaissance, ground-attack and even interception. When the Silver Birds were revived for one year only, in 1975, they naturally flew a set of four 105Ös.

KARO AS, AUSTRIAN AIR FORCE

In the same year that the Silver Birds flew again, 1975, a second Austrian team was also established flying four Saab 105Ös: Karo AS – Ace of Diamonds. Unlike the briefly revived Silver Birds, Karo AS would continue to perform demonstrations up to 1984.

▼ SAAB 105Ö

Saab 105Ö, A, Karo AS, Österreichische Luftstreitkräfte (Ace of Diamonds, Austrian Air Force), Brumowski airbase, Austria, 1980.
This aerobatic team performed more than 150 exhibitions from 1975 until 1984, both in Austria and abroad.

MODERN AEROBATIC TEAMS 007

MODERN AEROBATIC TEAMS — CHAPTER 1 – EUROPE

BELGIUM

▼ HAWKER HUNTER F.6
Hawker Hunter F.6, IF80, Diables Rouges/De Rode Duibel, Belgische Luchtmacht – Force Aérienne Belge (Red Devils, Belgian Air Force), Chièvres airbase, Belgium, 1960.
The team was founded in 1957 flying Hawker Hunters until 1963. Re-established in 1965, they flew Fouga Magisters until 1977.

▼ SIAI MARCHETTI SF 260
SIAI Marchetti SF 260, ST-03, Diables Rouges/De Rode Duibel, Belgische Luchtmacht – Force Aérienne Belge (Red Devils, Belgian Air Force), Beauvechain airbase, Belgium, 2014.
The team was re-formed in 2011, this time flying the SF 260.

▼ LOCKHEED F-104G STARFIGHTER
Lockheed F-104G Starfighter, FX90, 350 Squadron, 1st Wing, Slivers Demonstration Duo, Belgische Luchtmacht – Force Aérienne Belge (Belgian Air Force), Beauvechain airbase, Belgium, 1973.
The Duo flew the Starfighter from 1969 until 1975, being the first aerobatic team to use this aircraft.

RED DEVILS, BELGIAN AIR FORCE

Originally formed in 1957 from the 7th Fighter Wing, flying Hawker Hunter F.6s out of Chièvres airbase, the Red Devils are currently the Belgian Air Force's official aerobatic display team.

Two years after their formation, the team were staging displays with 16 aircraft but this was subsequently reduced to five for reasons of practicality. Having carried on for four more years, up to 1963, the team was then dissolved along with the 7th Fighter Wing. However, the Red Devils were revived in 1965, equipped with Fouga CM 170R Magister trainers. This new phase of the team's existence saw them performing all over Europe until a second dissolution in 1977, resulting from the Magister's retirement and replacement with Dassault/Dornier Alpha Jets. Sadly, budget constraints then ensured that there would be no Alpha Jet-flying Red Devils. However, 34 years later the team was revived for a second time, flying SIAI Marchetti SF 260 trainers which they continue to fly today.

SLIVERS DEMONSTRATION DUO, BELGIAN AIR FORCE

Alongside the Magister-flying Red Devils, the Belgian Air Force also operated a demonstration duo flying Lockheed F-104G Starfighters. The pilots chosen for this duty were Major Steve Nuyts and Adjutant Chef Palmer De Vlieger from 350 Squadron and their first performance was on May 14, 1969, during a graduation ceremony at Brustem airbase.

The duo's unusual name was based on a quote from Lockheed test pilot Glenn 'Snake' Reaves, who once described the F-104 as a 'Silver Sliver' due to its sharp and pointy profile. The Slivers' F-104 aircraft were painted in green and tan with grey undersides with the team logo on both intakes. The logo was dropped for 1972, apparently due to poor quality paint which caused it to fade very quickly, and the word 'Slivers' was added as a white inscription instead.

At the end of each display, the Slivers would cross just 2m apart at speeds ranging from 550-750km/h. The end came in July 1975 when Nuyts moved on to other duties and no replacement was apparent. The duo had reportedly made 68 performances across Belgium, the UK, France, West Germany and Italy.

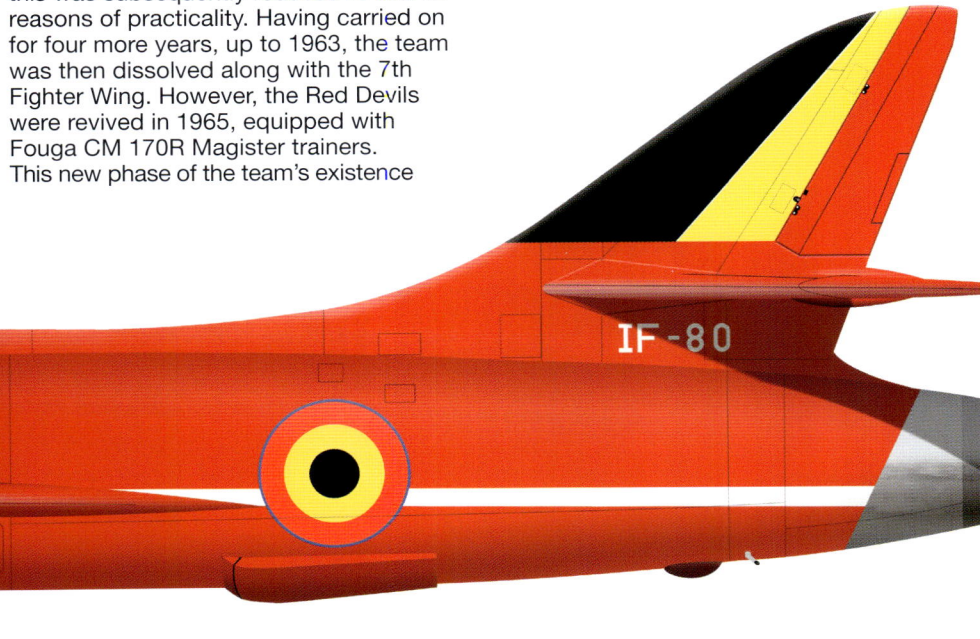

MODERN AEROBATIC TEAMS CHAPTER 1 – EUROPE

BELARUS

▼ AERO L-39C ALBATROS
Aero L-39C Albatros, Belaya Rus (White Rus), 07, 206th Training Centre for Aircrew, Air Force and Air Defence Forces of the Republic of Belarus, 116th Guards Assault Airbase, Lida, Belarus, 2018.
The team began operating in 2006.

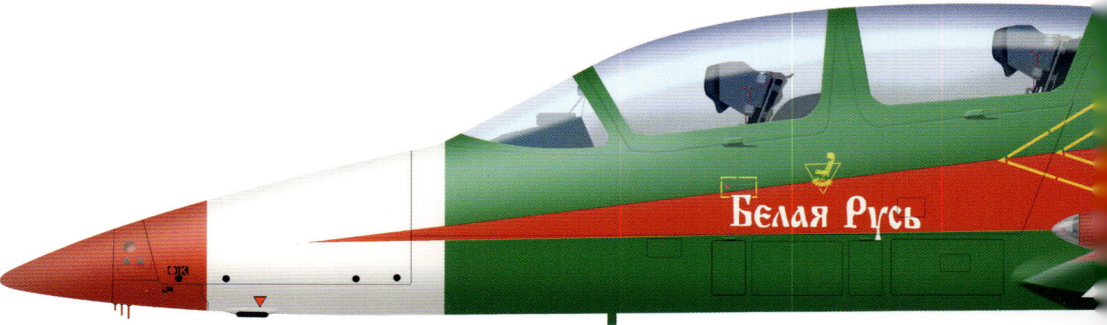

CROATIA

▼ PILATUS PC-9
Pilatus PC-9, 057, Krila Oluje, 392. eskadrila aviona, Hrvatsko ratno zrakoplovstvo (Wings of Storm, 392nd Aviation Squadron, Croatian Air Force), 93rd Air Force Base, Zadar, Croatia, 2013.
The team was disbanded in 2015 when all six pilots left the air force at once; it would be re-formed with new pilots, resuming flights the same year.

BELAYA RUS 2006

The Belarusian Air Force accepted its first two ex-Ukrainian Czech-built Aero L-39C Albatros advanced jet trainers on December 20, 2005, with another three arriving in January 2006 and a further five following for a total of ten. That same year, the Belaya Rus aerobatic team were formed as part of the 206th Flight Training Centre in Lida. The team fly six L-39s in red, white and green on special occasions, particularly during parades over Central Avenue in Minsk.

KRILA OLUJE, CROATIAN AIR FORCE

The Krila Oluje or 'Wings of Storm' are the Croatian Air Force's display team. They were formed in 2003 and are stationed at Zemunik airbase near Zadar, Croatia, the team's pilots being instructors with more than 600 flight hours.

While they fly six Pilatus PC-9Ms from a set of 20 bought back in 1996-7 (only 14 of which currently remain), the team evidently do not have six dedicated machines. Rather, they use whichever PC-9Ms happen to be available as required. If a pilot is ill or unavailable for any given show, there are no backups and the team will perform as a quintet instead.

Their first performance, with just four aircraft, was during the opening ceremony of the European sailing championship which took place in Zadar on July 23, 2004. The team were then officially presented to the public in 2005 and had grown to encompass five aircraft by the end of that year. The first six-strong formation was flown on March 25, 2009.

Meanwhile, one member of Krila Oluje from 2005-7, Captain Diana Doboš, had become only the third woman in the world to fly as part of an aerobatic team. In a highly unusual move, all six pilots of the team resigned from the Croatian Air Force on March 4, 2015 – effectively bringing Wings of Storm to an unscheduled conclusion. However, they were swiftly replaced and the re-formed team has been flying ever since.

MODERN AEROBATIC TEAMS **011**

MODERN AEROBATIC TEAMS CHAPTER 1 – EUROPE

CZECH REPUBLIC

ALCA DISPLAY TEAM, CZECH AIR FORCE
Developed from the Aero L-59 Super Albatros, the L-159A ALCA advanced jet trainer/light combat aircraft is flown by the appropriately-named ALCA Display Team duo. The team was formed in 2016 and their display takes place in two parts: the first third is a role demonstration accompanied by pyrotechnics on the ground while the remaining two thirds showcases the aircraft's outstanding handling qualities. To date, displays have taken place across Europe, including in the UK, France, Poland, Hungary, Lithuania, Slovakia and Slovenia.

DENMARK

BABY BLUE, ROYAL DANISH AIR FORCE
Formed during the mid-1980s by four ex-F-104 pilots-turned-instructors, Baby Blue ground to a halt after a few years when the original members moved on. However, when the Saab Draken was retired from Danish service in 1993 a number of ex-Draken pilots joined the Flyveskolen, the basic flight training school at Karup, as instructors. They were keen to revive Baby Blue and did so using Saab T-17 Supporter trainers.
The T-17 is the Danish version of the Swedish-made MFI-17, itself a military version of the civilian MFI-15 Safari – a high-wing side-by-side two-seater powered by a single air-cooled 200hp Lycoming IO-360-A1B6 flat-four piston engine. Baby Blue, apparently named after the original team's callsign, fly four T-17s and are a regular fixture at Danish airshows as well as, less frequently, shows abroad.

FINLAND

MIDNIGHT HAWKS, FINNISH AIR FORCE
With a history stretching right back to before the Second World War, the Midnight Hawks are the aerobatics team of the Finnish Air Force. Up to 1997, the team had no specific name. They did, however, have a very specific venue: the Finnish Air Force Training Air Wing's annual Midnight Sun Airshow which normally takes place on the third Friday in June when the sun is visible around the clock.
The show began as a traditional midsummer party for the wing's personnel, their families and the people of the nearby Kauhava village, including an airshow from around 7pm to midnight. This has since grown into an event which regularly attracts up to 20,000 people.
From 1960 to 1980, the unnamed team flew displays with both Saab 91 Safir piston engine trainers and Fouga Magister jets, swapping these for the Finnish-designed Valmet L-70 Vinka and the BAe Hawk Mk.51 respectively during the 1980s.
Then, during the 1990s, the team began making appearances beyond their airshow of origin – finally becoming the Midnight Hawks, based on four BAe Hawks, in 1997.

▼ AERO L-159 ALCA

Aero L-159 Alca, 6059, ALCA display Team, Vzdušné síly (Czech Air Force), Čáslav Airbase, Czech Republic, 2023.
The Czech Air Force has used a pair of L-159 ALCA aircraft as its display team since 2016.

▼ SAAB T-17 SUPPORTER

Saab T-17 Supporter, T-421, Baby Blue, Flyveskolen, Flyvevåbnet (Basic Flying School, Royal Danish Air Force), Avnø airbase, Denmark, 2022.
The Baby Blue aerobatic team got its name from the callsign used by the aircraft performing flybys, during the annual ceremonies to mark the liberation of the country, on May 4.

▼ BAE HAWK MK.51

BAe Hawk MK.51, HW-341/1, Midnight-Hawks, Hävittäjälentolaivue 41, Ilmasotakoulu, Ilmavoimat (No. 41 Fighter Squadron, Training Air Wing, Finnish Air Force), Jyväskylä Airport, Finland, 2022.
The pilots of the Midnight-Hawks are instructors at the Finnish Training Air Wing.

MODERN AEROBATIC TEAMS   013

MODERN AEROBATIC TEAMS — CHAPTER 1 – EUROPE

FRANCE

▼ DASSAULT MD450 OURAGAN
Dassault MD450 Ouragan, 155, Patrouille de France, Escadron de Chasse 3/4 'Flandre', SPA 160 'Diable Rouge', Armée de l'Air (Patrol of France, Fighter squadron 3/4, Flight 160 Red Devil, French Air Force), airbase 136, Bremgarten, West Germany, 1956.
During its early years, the team comprised aircraft and personnel from different units; the SPA 160 provided them in 1956.

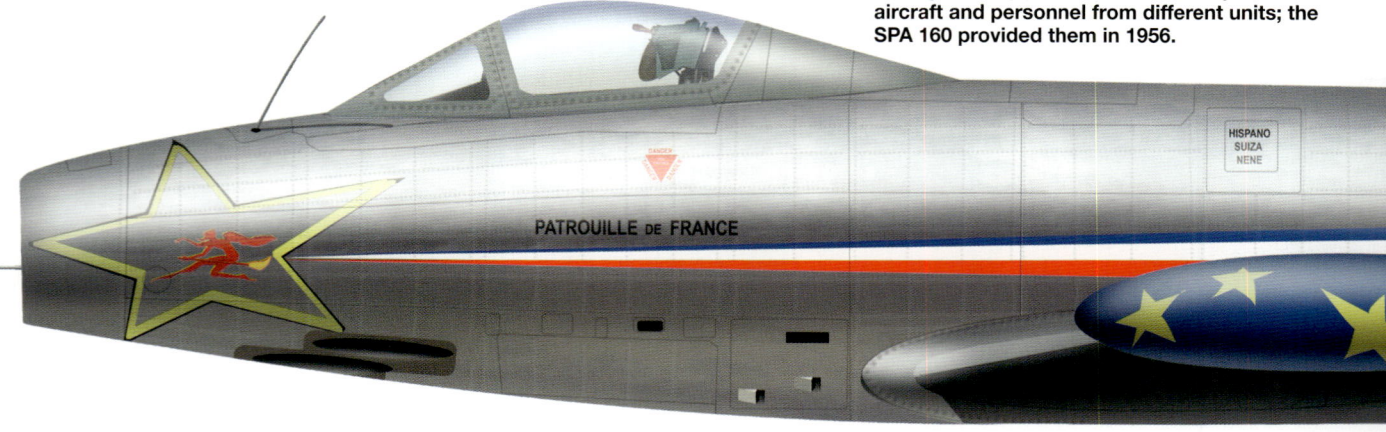

PATROUILLE DE FRANCE, FRENCH AIR FORCE

One of the oldest and most well-known teams in the world, Patrouille de France trace their beginnings back to 1931. They were officially commissioned in 1953 and flew Republic F-84G Thunderjets – albeit for just one year.

From 1954 through to 1981 they would successively be equipped with Dassault Ouragans (up to 1957), Dassault Mystère IVs (up to 1964) and Fouga Magisters (up to 1981). At that point they received by far their most enduring, iconic, and current, aircraft type: the Dassault-Breguet/Dornier Alpha Jet.

Today the team is composed of nine pilots plus a non-flying commander drawn from the fighter units of the French Air Force, with three volunteers joining and three existing members leaving every year. Displays are usually performed with eight aircraft, though the team has 12 Alpha Jets in total.

The team's callsign is Athos, with the leader being Athos 1. Athos 2 and 3 are first-year team members and Athos 4 is usually positioned behind the leader – taking their place when their year as No. 1 is up.

Athos 5 is the solo leader and Athos 6 is the second solo. Athos 7 and 8 are the 'exteriors', being usually positioned furthest from the leader. Athos 9 is the 'replacement' who can substitute for any team member except the leader. Logistical support for the team is provided by a Transall C-160, which carries several tons of equipment to each performance venue. The team celebrated their 70th anniversary in 2023 by staging their own airshow at their Salon-de-Provence base, just north of Marseille, with more than 100 aircraft attending, including the Patrouille Suisse, Croatia's Wings of Storm and the Saudi Hawks.

▼ DASSAULT MD454 MYSTERE IVA

Dassault MD454 Mystere IVA, 312, Patrouille de France, Armée de l'Air (Patrol of France, French Air Force), airbase 133, Nancy-Ochey, France, 1961. The Mystere IVA was used for seven years, starting in 1957.

MODERN AEROBATIC TEAMS **015**

MODERN AEROBATIC TEAMS — CHAPTER 1 – EUROPE

▼ FOUGA CM 170 MAGISTER

Fouga CM 170 Magister, Patrouille de France, Armée de l'Air (Patrol of France, French Air Force), airbase 701, Salon-de-Provence, France, 1978.
Patrouille de France flew the Magister for 16 years, from 1964 until 1981, replacing it with the Alpha Jet that year; this aircraft has the latter colour scheme (used from 1971 onwards).

▼ DASSAULT-BREGUET/DORNIER ALPHA JET E

Dassault-Breguet/Dornier Alpha Jet E, 1, Patrouille de France, Armée de l'Air (Patrol of France, French Air Force), airbase 701, Salon-de-Provence, France, 2021.
In 2021, celebrating the 75th anniversary of the publication of the Le Petit Prince by Antoine de Saint-Exupery, the team's aircraft had special markings applied to their fins.

MODERN AEROBATIC TEAMS 017

MODERN AEROBATIC TEAMS CHAPTER 1 – EUROPE

GERMANY

▼ FOUGA CM 170-1 MAGISTER
Fouga CM 170-1 Magister, AA-213, FFS A Aerobatic Team, FlugzeugFührerSchule, Luftwaffe (Aviation Pilots School A, German Air Force), Landsberg-Lech airbase, Germany, 1961.
From 1959 to 1961 the aircraft were flown by British instructors attached to the German FlugzeugFührerSchule A. They were then replaced by German pilots until the disbandment of the team the following year.

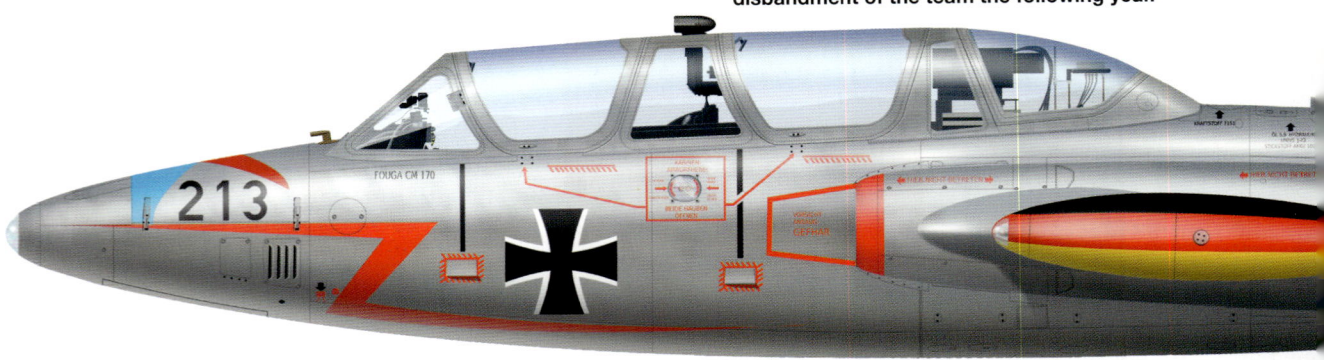

▼ LOCKHEED F-104G STARFIGHTER
Lockheed F-104G Starfighter, 26+72, Vikings, Marinefliegergeschwader 2, Marineflieger, Marine (Naval Aviation Squadron 2, Navy Air Arm, German Navy), Eggebek airbase, Germany, 1986.
The Vikings duo was awarded the prestigious AGL Trophy by the Aviation Group Leeuwarden in the Netherlands in 1986.

FFS A ACRO TEAM, GERMAN AIR FORCE
FFS B ACRO TEAM, GERMAN AIR FORCE

Four British flying instructors based at the German Air Force flying school, FlugzeugFührerSchule A (FFS A), helped to establish an aerobatic team for the West German Luftwaffe towards the end of 1959. The team, led by Squadron Leader Raymond Hoggarth and unofficially known as FFS A Acro Team, started training in April 1960 using four Fouga CM 170R Magisters. Their display debut was on April 24, 1960, at Reutlingen, with performances at Kempten and Landsberg following.

Hoggarth stayed on for 1961 but German pilots were recruited for the other three positions and the aircraft were given a colour scheme based on the German flag. More displays followed until the team was disbanded following a final display at Offenburg on May 27, 1962. A second team flying Lockheed T-33A trainers was formed at FlugzeugFührerSchule B (FFS B), stationed at Fürstenfeldbruck, in 1962 but this would prove to be short-lived.

VIKINGS DUO, WEST GERMAN NAVY

An aerobatic duo flying F-104s was formed in 1979 from Marinefliegergeschwader 2 but was soon disbanded following a crash during a non-aerobatic flight. Four years later, the same pilots returned as the Vikings for a show on August 14, 1983, at their home base of Eggebeck. The aircraft wore the standard West German Navy scheme of grey and light grey and the show lasted just eight minutes.

In 1984, however, a second duo was stood up alongside the first – also known as the Vikings – so that 'the Vikings' could literally perform in two places at once. The team toured across the USA and Canada in August 1986 and when they got home their aircraft were repainted in a new white, blue and red scheme. However, both duos were disbanded on September 27, 1986, when the West German Navy retired the F-104.

▼ LOCKHEED T-33A

Lockheed T-33A, AB-750, FFS B Aerobatic Team, FlugzeugFührerSchule B, Luftwaffe (Aviation Pilots School B, German Air Force), Fürstenfeldbruck airbase, Germany, 1962. This team performed for a short time until a tragic accident in May 1962 led to a ban of aerobatic flying in the Luftwaffe.

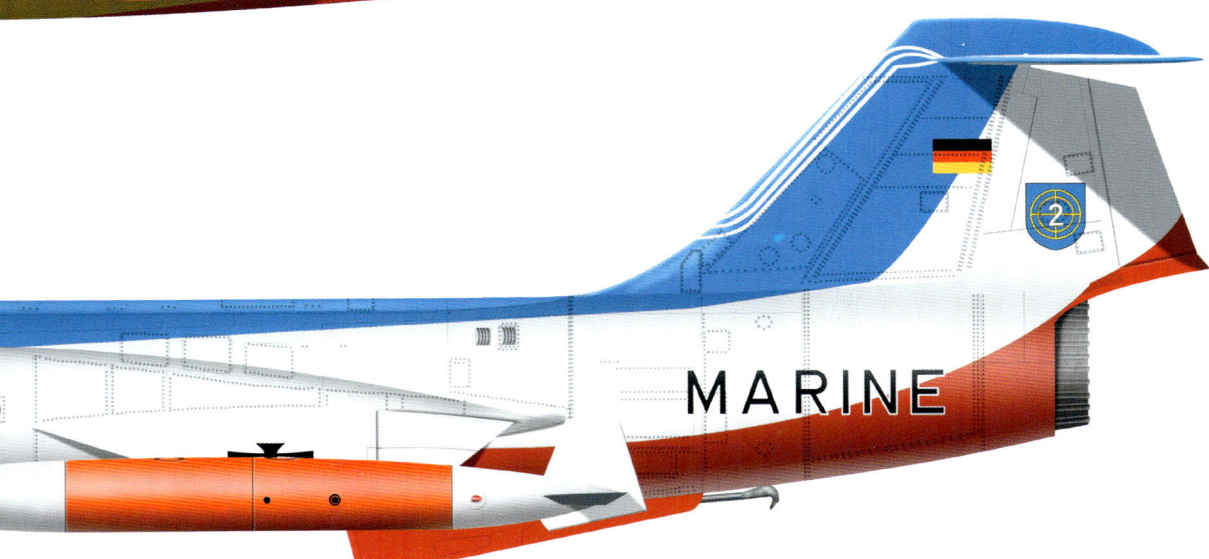

MODERN AEROBATIC TEAMS **019**

MODERN AEROBATIC TEAMS — CHAPTER 1 – EUROPE

GREECE

HUNGARY

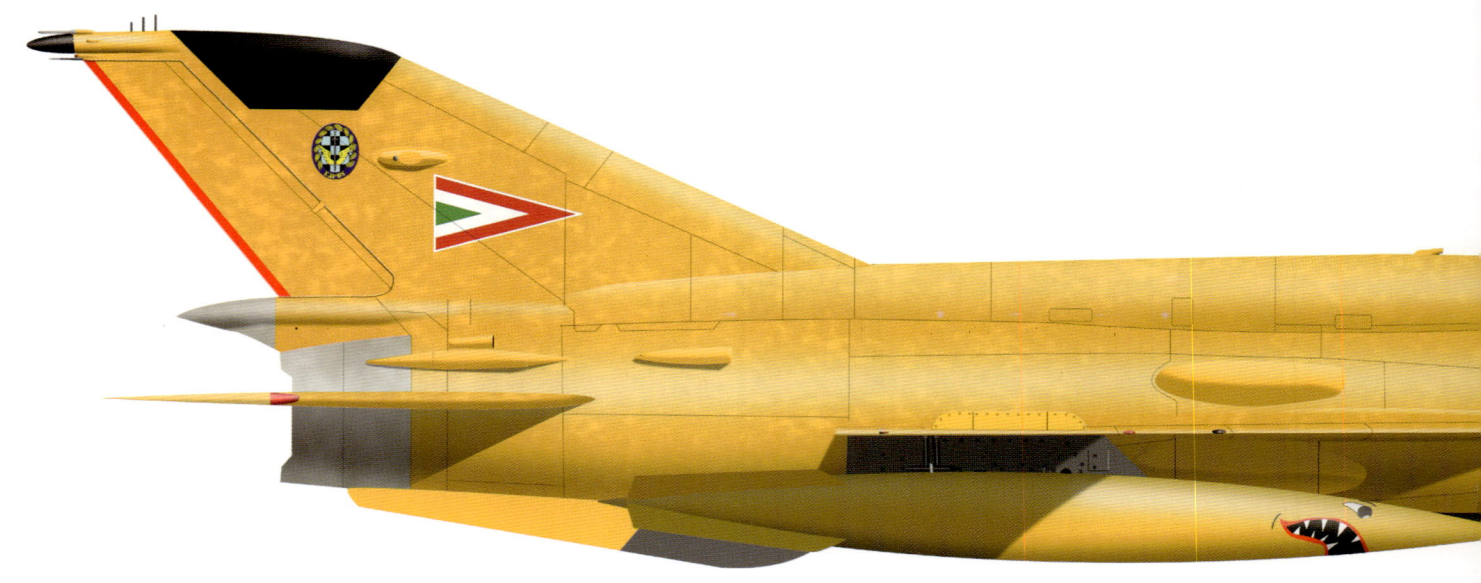

▼ REPUBLIC F-84G THUNDERJET

Republic F-84G Thunderjet, 998, Aces Four, 337 Mira, Polemikí Aeroporía (337 Squadron, Hellenic Air Force), Larissa airbase, Greece, 1956.
Created by the commander of the 337th Squadron in secrecy in 1952, the team received official recognition soon afterwards and performed until the Hellenic Air Force converted to the F-86 in 1957.

▼ NORTHROP F-5A FREEDOM FIGHTER

Northrop F-5A Freedom Fighter, 69135, New Hellenic Flame, 337 Mira, Polemikí Aeroporía (337 Squadron, Hellenic Air Force), Larissa airbase, Greece, 1967.
New Hellenic Flame was set up in 337 Mira flying the F-5A, but performed only two shows before being disbanded.

▼ MIKOYAN MIG-21BIS FISHBED

Mikoyan MiG-21bis Fishbed, 1904, Capeti, égi huszárok, Magyar Légierő (Sky Hussars, Hungarian Air Force), Taszár airbase Hungary, 1993.
The Hungarian Air Force participated in several air shows with a team of four MiG-21s, including one painted in an overall yellow colour scheme; the others featuring tactical camouflage colours.

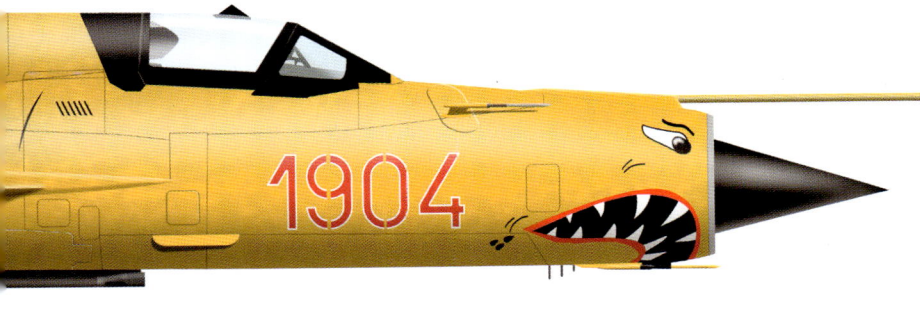

ACES FOUR, HELLENIC AIR FORCE

The commander of the Hellenic Air Force's 337th Pursuit-Bombing Squadron in early 1952, Lieutenant Colonel Kokas, was inspired to form the first Greek display team after watching the USAF's Skyblazers team perform.

Concerned that his commanders might take a dim view of using four expensive F-84G fighters for aerobatics, Kokas evidently recruited three other pilots and attempted to train in secret. However, word soon reached those in authority and ultimately the team were given approval to continue. The name Aces Four was chosen, the Thunderjets were painted dark blue and the team was attached to the Larissa-based 110th Air Wing.

The team then moved to Elefsina airbase in 1956 and gave a performance that same year in Milan, Italy. During the following year, the team trained to take-off and land in formation and reportedly managed to tighten their manoeuvres to a minimum separation distance of just 1m between the aircraft.

The end came in August 1957 when the Hellenic Air Force replaced their F-84Gs with Canadair CL-13A Sabre Mk.2s – and the Aces Four were no more.

HELLENIC FLAME, HELLENIC AIR FORCE

The Aces Four might have been gone but in 1958 the Hellenic Air Force stood up another display team: Hellenic Flame. Naturally, they were equipped with Sabres – first five of them, then seven. Over the next six years they appeared at displays across Greece as well as in France, Italy, Turkey and West Germany, disbanding in September 1964.

This was not the end of the story, however, as the team re-formed in 1967 as part of 337 Squadron under the name New Hellenic Flame. They were equipped with Northrop F-5A Freedom Fighters but managed only two performances before disbanding.

SKY HUSSARS, HUNGARIAN AIR FORCE

During the cold war, the Hungarian People's Army Air Force was equipped with a variety of Soviet-made aircraft – including numerous MiGs. When the Soviet Union fractured and fell apart, the air force put forward the idea of establishing a display team using a trio of MiG-21bis fighters as the Sky Hussars. The team made its first performance in 1991, with one of the aircraft painted yellow to represent an 'enemy'.

Expanded to four aircraft – three in camouflage, the last in yellow – the team gave their final performance in front of a large audience at the Royal International Air Tattoo (RIAT), Fairford, UK, in 1993.

MODERN AEROBATIC TEAMS **021**

MODERN AEROBATIC TEAMS — CHAPTER 1 – EUROPE

IRELAND

▼ PILATUS PC-9M

Pilatus PC-9M, 264, Silver Swallows, Air Corps College, Flying Training School, Irish Air Corps, Casement Aerodrome, Dublin, Republic of Ireland, 2022.
Following a hiatus of more than 20 years, the Silver Swallows returned to operations, this time flying the Pilatus PC-9M. The aircraft carry markings celebrating the 100th anniversary of the Irish Air Corps.

▼ FOUGA CM 170 MAGISTER

Fouga CM 170 Magister, 220, Silver Swallows, Light Strike Squadron, Irish Air Corps, Casement Aerodrome, Dublin, Republic of Ireland, 1996.
The team made its debut performance in 1982 for the 60th anniversary of the creation of the Air Corps. Disbanded in 1998, when the Magister was withdrawn from service, the team was reformed in 2022 using the Pilatus PC-9.

SILVER SWALLOWS, IRISH AIR CORPS

Formed from the Irish Air Corps Light Strike Squadron, this team initially flew four silver-painted Fouga CM 170 Magisters to celebrate the 60th anniversary of the corps in 1982. Based at Casement Aerodrome, Baldonnel, near Dublin, they continued into 1983 – incorporating a formation loop into their display. They eventually received the official Silver Swallows name in August 1987.

Mostly performing only in Ireland, the team did venture abroad for the first time to perform at the RAF Brawdy Open Day event on July 26, 1990. Further international show appearances eventually followed in the UK and Belgium in 1997 to celebrate the 75th anniversary of the corps. The following year, when the Magister was retired from service in Ireland, the team was disbanded.

The Silver Swallows made a surprising comeback in 2022, however, with instructors from the Air Corps College, Flying Training School flying four Pilatus PC-9Ms. Their first show was on July 10, 2022, and their first full display was at the 2022 RIAT.

TEAM WARRIOR, IRISH AIR CORPS

During the long hiatus of the Silver Swallows, the Irish Air Corps briefly formed another aerobatic team – this time under the name Team Warrior. Flying either three or four SIAI Marchetti SF 260WE Warrior trainers, they performed in Ireland during the early 2000s but never made an appearance abroad.

▼ SIAI MARCHETTI SF.260W

SIAI Marchetti SF.260W, 230, Team Warrior, Air Corps College, Flying Training School, Irish Air Corps, Casement Aerodrome, Dublin, Republic of Ireland, 2002.
Created in the early 2000s, the team used SF 260 aircraft from the Air Corps College painted in standard colours.

MODERN AEROBATIC TEAMS **023**

MODERN AEROBATIC TEAMS — CHAPTER 1 – EUROPE

ITALY

▼ CANADAIR CL-13 MK.4 SABRE

Canadair CL-13 Mk.4 Sabre, Frecce Tricolori, Pattuglia Acrobatica Nazionale, 313. Gruppo Addestramento Acrobatico, Aeronautica Militare (Tricolor Arrows, National Aerobatic Patrol, 313rd Aerobatic Training Group, Italian Air Force), Rivolto airbase, Italy, 1961.
This Sabre has the first colour scheme used by the team.

▼ AERMACCHI MB-339PAN

Aermacchi MB-339PAN, MM55059/ 5, Frecce Tricolori, Pattuglia Acrobatica Nazionale, 313. Gruppo Addestramento Acrobatico (Tricolor Arrows, National Aerobatic Patrol, 313rd Aerobatic Training Group) Aeronautica Militare (Italian Air Force), Rivolto airbase, Italy, 1961.
The Frecce Tricolori have flown the MB-339PAN since 1982, replacing the former Fiat G.91PAN. The team sadly was involved in a tragic accident in 1988 at Ramstein airbase, West Germany.

024 MODERN AEROBATIC TEAMS

FRECCE TRICOLORI, ITALIAN AIR FORCE

Ranking among the most famous of modern aerobatics teams, Italy's Frecce Tricolori were formally established on March 1, 1961, at Rivolto airbase in Udine as the successor to numerous earlier teams.

They had the full official title of 313th Acrobatic Training Group, National Aerobatic Team (PAN) Frecce Tricolori and were initially equipped with six F-86 Sabres. A further four were added for a total of nine plus a solo but these were all replaced in 1964 by new Fiat G.91 fighter-bombers. The Ginas had a good run – lasting 18 years in service – before being replaced by the team's current aircraft, the Aermacchi MB-339 A/PAN MLU in 1982. Unfortunately, six years later, on August 28, 1988, the team were involved in one of the worst airshow disasters in history – at Ramstein airbase in West Germany. Their ten aircraft were performing a manoeuvre known as the Cardioide or 'pierced heart' when three collided. One of the aircraft came down on the runway in a fireball which engulfed a spectator area before coming to rest against an ice cream van. Another of the team's aircraft crashed onto a UH-60 helicopter, fatally injuring its pilot, and the third disintegrated in midair before coming down as a hail of debris along the runway. A total of 70 people died – 67 spectators and three pilots – and 346 spectators suffered serious injuries. Despite this tragedy, the team were brought back up to full strength and continued to perform – clocking 50,000 flying hours on the Aermacchi MB-339 in 2000. Efforts were made to get the MB-339s replaced with Aermacchi M-345 HETs (High-Efficiency Trainers) in 2013 and again in 2016, then once again in 2020. In September 2024, the team's next aircraft was unveiled: the Alenia Aermacchi M-346 Master.

MODERN AEROBATIC TEAMS **025**

MODERN AEROBATIC TEAMS — CHAPTER 1 – EUROPE

▼ REPUBLIC F-84F THUNDERSTREAK

Republic F-84F Thunderstreak, 5-619, Pattuglia Acrobatica Getti Tonanti, 5ª Aerobrigata, Aeronautica Militare (Thunder Jets aerobatic team, 5th Air Brigade, Italian Air Force), Rimini Miramare airbase, Italy, 1960.
Each aircraft of the team was painted in one of the colours of the Olympic rings, when they performed at the inauguration of the 1960 Rome Olympics.

▼ REPUBLIC F-84G THUNDERJET

Republic F-84G Thunderjet, 51-61, Pattuglia Acrobatica Tigri Bianche, 51ª Aerobrigata, Aeronautica Militare (White Tigers aerobatic Team, 51st Air Brigade, Italian Air Force), Istrana airbase, Veneto, Italy, 1955.
The Tigri Bianche was a short-lived aerobatic team, performing for only a year from 1955 to 1956.

TIGRI BIANCHE, ITALIAN AIR FORCE

A number of aerobatic display teams emerged from the Italian Air Force prior to the creation of Frecce Tricolori – one of them being Tigri Bianche (White Tigers). Formed in 1955 from the 51st Aerobrigata at Istrana airbase, they lasted only a year. During that time, however, flying F-84G Thunderjets, they became the first Italian aerobatics team to tour North America.

GETTI TONANTI, ITALIAN AIR FORCE

Three years after the dissolution of the Tigri Bianche, and two years before the creation of the Frecce Tricolori, the Getti Tonanti (Thunder Jets) were formed in 1959. They flew five F-84F Thunderstreaks with different-coloured tails and 'Getti Tonanti' painted in large characters on their noses. While they too only existed for a year, their finest hour came in August 1960 when the jets were repainted in bright colours for the opening of the Summer Olympics in Rome.

MODERN AEROBATIC TEAMS **027**

MODERN AEROBATIC TEAMS CHAPTER 1 – EUROPE

NETHERLANDS

DASH FOUR, ROYAL NETHERLANDS AIR FORCE

Like many other teams of the period, when Royal Netherlands Air Force pilots at Soesterberg airbase began aerobatics training on January 4, 1956, they lacked a catchy name. This state of affairs continued for months and the still-unnamed F-84F-equipped team gave their first public display at Leeuwarden on July 14, 1956. Within a fortnight, their aircraft had received a fresh paint job reminiscent of that worn by the USAF's Thunderbirds with white, red and blue highlights over a natural metal finish.

▼ REPUBLIC F-84F THUNDERSTREAK

Republic F-84F Thunderstreak, Dash Four, Koninklijke Luchtmacht (Royal Netherlands Air Force), Soesterberg airbase, Netherlands, 1956. This aircraft is painted in the first colour scheme used by the team. In 1959 when it performed in the USA, the team flew with borrowed USAF Thunderstreaks.

▶ AÉROSPATIALE ALOUETTE III

Aérospatiale Alouette III, A-246, Grasshoppers, 300 Squadron, Koninklijke Luchtmacht (Royal Netherlands Air Force), Deelen airbase, Netherlands, 1979.
The Grasshoppers' helicopters were painted in this striped colour scheme in 1979. The team would perform from 1973 until 1995.

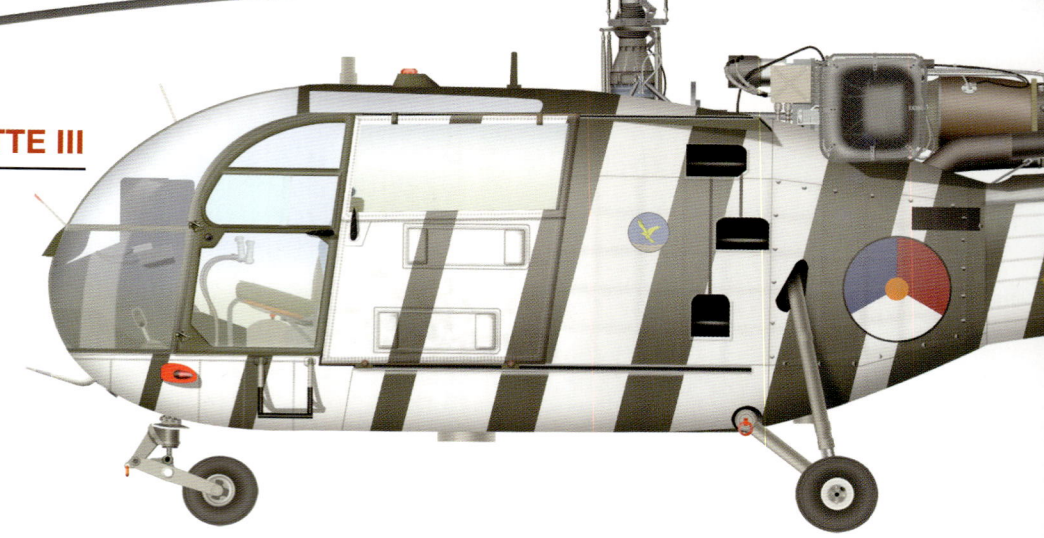

Eventually the team received the name Dash Four but the paint was stripped for the 1957 season – leaving the aircraft in all-over bare metal, though they were also now fitted with white smoke generators. The aircraft were then given colourful highlights for a second time. However, they were left behind in March 1959 when the team's pilots took up an invitation to fly at the World Congress of Flight event in Las Vegas – since they had been promised the use of USAF aircraft.

There was an incident on April 9 when two of these aircraft, flown by Dash Four pilots and painted with orange highlights, collided during practice but both men survived and the performance took place as planned from April 12-15. Back in the Netherlands, the team's final performance was on June 19, 1959.

GRASSHOPPERS, ROYAL NETHERLANDS AIR FORCE

Four pilots flying Aérospatiale Alouette III helicopters with the RNLAF's 299 Squadron at Deelen airbase decided to compose a demonstration routine to celebrate the RNLAF's 60th anniversary in 1973. They quickly came up with the name 'Grasshoppers' and their machines were painted in dark matt green with yellow highlights. Following their initial demo, their first display was on June 5, 1974, during an air force event at Duindigt.

Their first performance abroad was at USAFE Hahn airbase in West Germany in 1978 and in 1979 the team's aircraft were repainted with a pattern of slightly slanted vertical white stripes. By this point 299 Squadron was converting to Bo 105C helicopters so the team were transferred to 300 Squadron instead.

The Grasshoppers' paint scheme changed again for 1980 – the helicopters becoming white, red and blue all over and being fitted with smoke generators. Retirement beckoned in 1995, when the Alouette III was finally phased out of RNLAF service.

WHISKEY FOUR, ROYAL NETHERLANDS AIR FORCE

At around the same time that the soon-to-be Dash Four team was being established, a second unnamed team was being formed at the RNLAF's Woensdrecht airbase and flight training school. The four pilots were all instructors and initially flew Gloster Meteors, these being swapped for new Lockheed T-33A trainers in 1958.

At first the team's aircraft had no special markings and although experiments were conducted with smoke this wasn't incorporated into their routine. After four years, in 1962, the team finally got their name: Whiskey Four. This was derived in straightforward fashion from the flight school's 'Whiskey' callsign and the number of aircraft in the squad. That same year, the team flew their first international displays in England and Scotland.

Their fame grew and in 1964 they were involved in the filming of a TV show and gave performances at airshows in both Belgium and Italy. Unfortunately, two of the team's T-33As collided during an airshow over their home base on June 8, 1965, killing both pilots.

New recruits were brought in and the team continued to fly in 1966, with the aircraft getting new white and green markings. However, it was becoming clear that all the T-33As were needed for training and the team had been disbanded by the end of the year. Pilots from 314 Squadron at Welschap airbase created a new Whiskey Four using their F-84Fs, painted white and green, in 1967. They flew for a short while but a pilot was then killed when his aircraft crashed during a practice flight and the last Whiskey Four was dissolved.

▼ LOCKHEED T-33A

Lockheed T-33A, M-52/ 51-6953, Whiskey Four, Koninklijke Luchtmacht (Royal Netherlands Air Force), Woensdrecht airbase, Netherlands, 1966. Formed in 1956, the team flew Gloster Meteors before transitioning to the T-33 in 1958. A new Whiskey Four emerged in 1967 flying F-84F. The four Xs on the tail are made with silhouettes of T-33s.

MODERN AEROBATIC TEAMS **029**

MODERN AEROBATIC TEAMS — CHAPTER 1 – EUROPE

NORWAY

▼ SAAB MFI-15 SAFARI
Saab MFI-15 Safari, 846/3, 'Yogi', Yellow Sparrows, Luftforsvarets flygeskole, Luftforsvaret (Air Force Flight Training School, Royal Norwegian Air Force), Bardufoss Air Station, Norway, 2015. Besides its role as the primary flight trainer for the RnoAF, the Saab Safari is used by the team for aerial exhibitions.

POLAND

030 MODERN AEROBATIC TEAMS

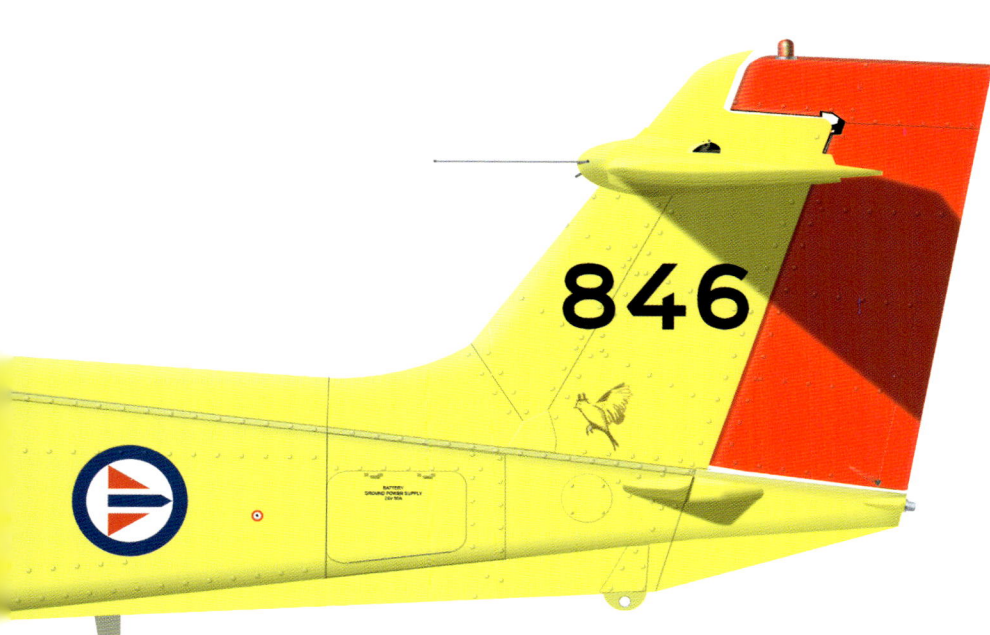

YELLOW SPARROWS, ROYAL NORWEGIAN AIR FORCE

The Royal Norwegian Air Force bought 25 Saab MFI-15 Safaris in 1981 for basic pilot training then supplemented these with four MFI-17 Supporters in 1987. The RNoAF's official aerobatic display team, the Yellow Sparrows, are based at Bardufoss airbase and have displayed between four and six of these aircraft at shows across Europe since at least 2015.

Each aircraft retains its standard RNoAF colours: bright yellow with an orange rudder, under-nose panel and wingtips, plus a small 'sparrow' logo on the fin. On some occasions the No. 1 aircraft has also been painted with a sharkmouth on the under-nose panel.

The aircraft are sometimes seen adorned with callsigns too: 'Surf', 'Yogi', 'Plates', 'Sailor' and 'Hotdog'. These are transferred from aircraft to aircraft but the Safaris often appear without them.

▼ **PZL-130 TC-II ORLIK**

PZL-130 TC-II Orlik, 029, Orlik, Siły Powietrzne (Eagle, Polish Air Force), Radom-Sadków airbase, Poland, 2019. Named after the indigenous trainer it flies, the team was created in 1998. The Orlik team's aircraft are flown in the standard colours of the PZL-130 fleet. This aircraft has a smoke dispenser pod attached to the underside of the rear fuselage.

ORLIK AEROBATIC TEAM, POLISH AIR FORCE

Flying Polish-made turboprop-powered PZL-130 Orlik trainers, the Polish Air Force's aerobatic display team was formed in 1998 and named after the aircraft (Orlik meaning 'Eagle' in English). Their first performance was on April 15, 1998, in Poland and their first international performance was at RIAT in the UK that same year.

Initially consisting of just four aircraft, the team was expanded to seven at the end of 2000 and has since flown some displays with nine. All team members are volunteers drawn from the 42nd Training Air Base at Radom-Sadków.

MODERN AEROBATIC TEAMS **031**

MODERN AEROBATIC TEAMS CHAPTER 1 – EUROPE
PORTUGAL

▼ CESSNA T-37C

Cessna T-37C, 2406, Asas de Portugal, Esquadra 102, Força Aérea Portuguesa (Wings of Portugal, 102 Squadron, Portuguese Air Force), airbase 1, Sintra, Portugal, 1980.
Initially created to represent the Portuguese Air Force at the 1977 Royal Air Tattoo, the team would perform in many domestic and international air shows until its initial disbandment in 1992.

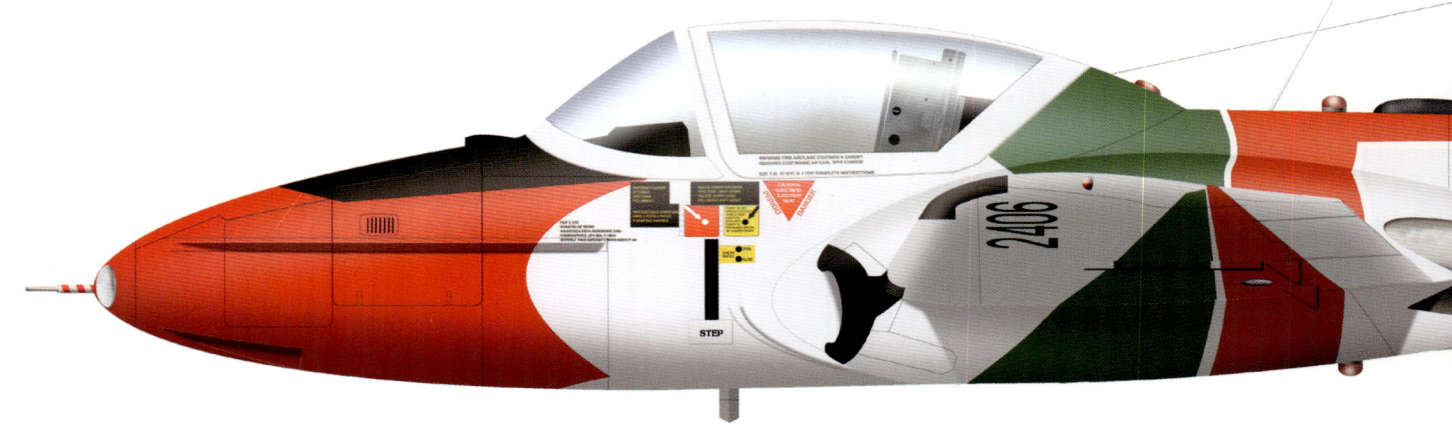

ASAS DE PORTUGAL, PORTUGUESE AIR FORCE

It was decided in 1977 that an aerobatic team should be formed to represent the Portuguese Air Force at that year's RIAT in the UK – resulting in the establishment of the Asas de Portugal or 'Wings of Portugal'. Drawn from 102 Squadron, the team flew six Cessna T-37C trainers painted in red, green and white colours. Over the next 15 years they participated in 146 airshows, 40 of them in foreign countries.

In 1992, however, the T-37 was retired from Portuguese service and the team was consequently disbanded. The following year, Germany transferred 50 Alpha Jets to Portugal in retrospective payment for German use of Beja airbase from 1964-1993.

Four years later, on June 27, 1997, the Asas de Portugal were revived as part of 103 Squadron at Beja – flying Alpha Jets, although not in special colours. The team lasted only a year this time before being disbanded.

However, a second revival followed in 2005 with the renewed team flying a pair of Alpha Jets in the classic white, red and green colours.

ROTORES DE PORTUGAL, PORTUGUESE AIR FORCE

Surprisingly the fixed-wing flying Asas de Portugal were preceded by a helicopter display team – the Rotores de Portugal having been formed a year earlier, in April 1976.

Established as part of 33 Squadron, they were based at Sintra airbase and made their first performance there flying four Alouette IIIs. The team gave their last display as a quartet in October 1980 and reduced to just two machines in 1982, simultaneously becoming part of 552 Squadron.

A further switch, to 111 Squadron, came about in 1991 and the team's complement rose again to become a trio of Alouette IIIs. Fourteen years later, in 2005, they rejoined 552 Squadron before being stood down in 2010 following the retirement of their helicopters.

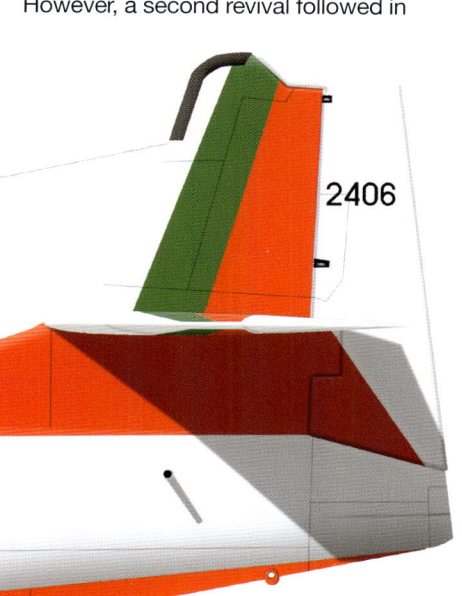

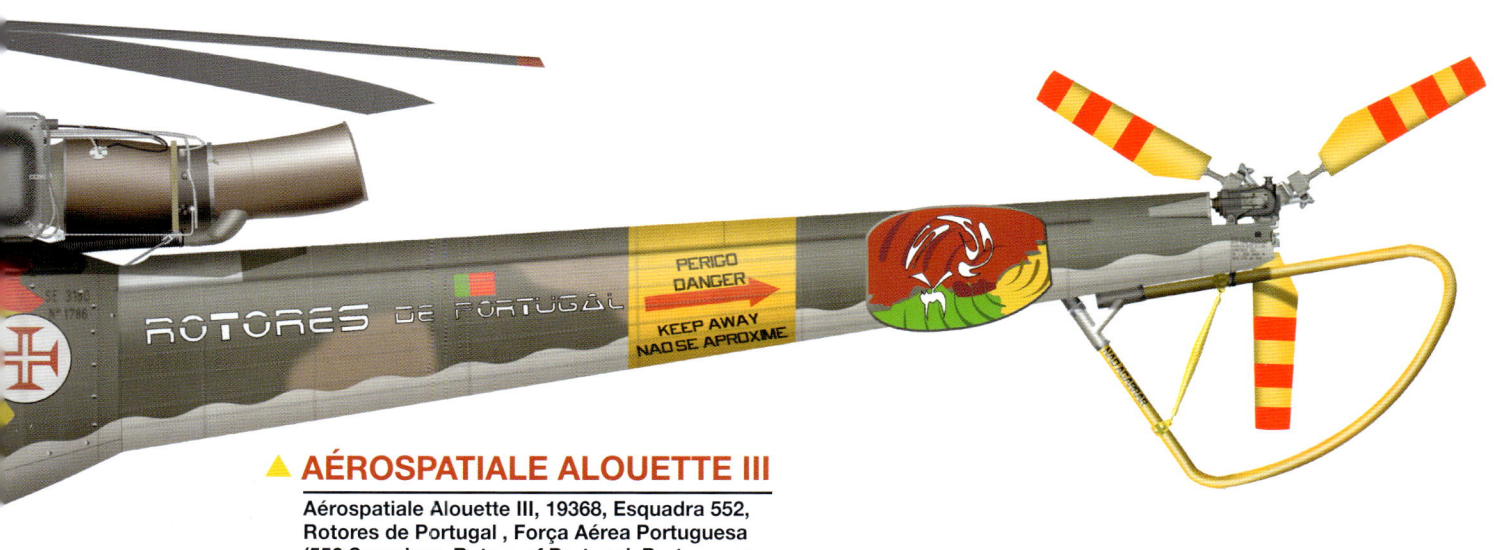

▲ AÉROSPATIALE ALOUETTE III

Aérospatiale Alouette III, 19368, Esquadra 552, Rotores de Portugal, Força Aérea Portuguesa (552 Squadron, Rotors of Portugal, Portuguese Air Force), airbase 11, Beja, Portugal, 2010.
The team would be located at several bases and within different units throughout their career; the last unit would be 552 Squadron in Beja prior to its disbandment in 2010.

MODERN AEROBATIC TEAMS **033**

MODERN AEROBATIC TEAMS — CHAPTER 1 – EUROPE

▼ DASSAULT-BREGUET-DORNIER ALPHA JET A

Dassault-Breguet-Dornier Alpha Jet A, 15250, Asas de Portugal, Esquadra 103, Força Aérea Portuguesa (Wings of Portugal, 103 Squadron, Portuguese Air Force), airbase 11, Beja, Portugal, 2007. The Asas de Portugal would be reformed in 2005, this time flying a duo of Alpha Jets.

PATRUHA SAO JORGE, PORTUGUESE AIR FORCE

A display team known as Dragoes or 'Dragons' was formed by the Portuguese Air Force in 1956, equipped with F-84 Thunderjets. However, this team was 'killed' in 1958 and replaced by a new team known as Sao Jorge or 'Saint George'. Stationed at the B.A.2 airbase in Ota, they initially flew four green F-84Gs with red highlights. This scheme was quickly replaced with a black upper/red lower design before the team's disbandment in 1961.

▼ REPUBLIC F-84G THUNDERJET

Republic F-84G Thunderjet, 5184, Patrulha São Jorge, Esquadra 21, Força Aérea Portuguesa (Saint George Patrol, 20 Squadron, Portuguese Air Force), airbase 2, Ota, Portugal, 1958.
The F-84s of the team were painted in a simple but striking black and red colour scheme.

MODERN AEROBATIC TEAMS **035**

MODERN AEROBATIC TEAMS CHAPTER 1 – EUROPE

RUSSIA

▼ SUKHOI SU-27 FLANKER
Sukhoi Su-27 Flanker, 12, Russkie Vityazi, Voenno-vozdushnye sily Rossii (Russian Knights, Russian Air Force), Kubinka, Russia 1993.
The team was formed in 1991 and has flown the Flanker since, in several versions. Three aircraft were involved in an accident while en route in Vietnam in 1995.

RUSSIAN KNIGHTS, RUSSIAN AIR FORCE

The Russian Knights aerobatic display team was formed on April 5, 1991, at Kubinka airbase from the 237th Guards Proskurov Aircraft Demonstration Centre. They were equipped with six Sukhoi Su-27s – a mix of two-seaters and single-seaters – and made their first international appearance at Scampton in the UK during September 1991.

They have since appeared in shows all over the world, from the USA to France, the Netherlands, Canada, Belgium, Slovatkia, Luxembourg, China, the United Arab Emirates, Finland, Bahrain, India, Hungary and beyond.

Three Russian Knights aircraft were destroyed, and four pilots killed, on December 12, 1995, when they flew into a mountain in Vietnam in dense fog – the worst disaster in the team's history.

The team later acquired a number of Su-30SMs and, in November 2019, began to receive the latest Su-35S fighters. In July 2020, the team gave a performance at Kubinka flying all three types in a single formation.

The team's last known appearance at the time of writing was in Dubai in November 2023. At the beginning of 2024 it was reported that Russian Knights-liveried Su-35 aircraft had begun conducting combat patrols and escort duties connected to the war in Ukraine. And in May 2024, it was further reported that an Su-27 in Russian Knights colours had been destroyed on the ground at Kushchyovskaya airbase by Ukrainian drones.

SWIFTS, RUSSIAN AIR FORCE

On May 6, 1991, shortly after the formation of the Su-27-flying Russian Knights, another team flying MiG-29s was formed at Kubinka: the Swifts.

Part of the 234th Guards Proskurov Aviation Regiment, the Swifts had a complement of six aircraft and initially only flew demonstrations that were closed to the public. Their first public display was in May 1992 at Reims airbase in France. After seven years, the most of the team's pilots retired and the team itself was disbanded in 1999.

However, the following year it was reinstated with new pilots but only four aircraft. This soon increased back to six, however. It was reported in 2018 that the team would be transitioning to Su-35s but this does not appear to have happened. Their last known performance, still flying MiG-29s, was at the opening of the International Maritime Defense Show, near St Petersburg, in June 2023.

▼ MIKOYAN MIG-29 FULCRUM

Mikoyan MiG-29 Fulcrum, 43, Strizhi, Voenno-vozdushnye sily Rossii, (Swifts, Russian Air Force), Kubinka, Russia 1993.
The Swifts were formed in 1990; this was the original colour scheme.

MODERN AEROBATIC TEAMS 037

MODERN AEROBATIC TEAMS   CHAPTER 1 – EUROPE

SLOVAKIA

▼ AERO L-39C ALBATROS

Aero L-39C Albatros, 0442/0, Biele Albatrosy, Vzdušné sily Ozbrojených síl Slovenskej republiky, (White Albatrosses, Slovakian Air Force), Košice airbase, Slovakia, 1993.
The team was formed in 1991, at the time still part of the Czechoslovakian Air Force; in 1993, with the independence of Slovakia, the team became part of the new air force.

SPAIN

▼ CASA C-101 AVIOJET/E.25

CASA C-101 Aviojet/E.25, 79-12/8 Patrulla-Águila, Ejército del Aire y del Espacio (Eagle Patrol, Spanish Air Force), San Javier airbase, Spain, 2018.
The team was created within the Spanish Air Force Academy and has always used the locally-made CASA C-101 aircraft; this particular example wears a badge commemorating the 75th anniversary of the Air Force Academy.

PATRULLA ÁGUILA, SPANISH AIR FORCE

The aerobatic demonstration team of the Spanish Air Force, Patrulla Águila or 'Eagle Patrol' was formed on July 4, 1985, flying seven CASA C-101 Aviojet advanced jet trainers – the type having been introduced five years earlier. The team are stationed at San Javier airbase in Spain's Murcia region and evidently have 12 C-101s on their books, although they only ever use seven of them, or occasionally six, for displays. In addition to 11 pilots, who are all flight instructors at the Air Force Academy, the team also have 30 ground personnel – of whom 16 are technicians who travel with

▼ NORTH AMERICAN F-86F SABRE

North American F-86F Sabre, 1-175/ C5-175, Patrulla Ascua, Ala 11, Ejército del Aire (Ember Patrol, Wing 11, Spanish Air Force), Manises airbase, Spain, 1962.
The team was officially named Patrulla Ascua in 1958 but had already existed for about two years by then; this aircraft displays the later colour scheme used from 1957 until disbandment in 1965.

038   MODERN AEROBATIC TEAMS

BIELE ALBATROSY, SLOVAKIAN AIR FORCE

The opening of the 9th World Parachuting Championship at Lucenec-Bolkovce airfield in Slovakia on August 3, 1991, saw the debut of a new aerobatic team: Biele Albatrosy or the 'White Albatrosses'.

Part of the Czechoslovakian Air Force's 2nd Air Training Regiment, based at Kosice, they flew three smoke generator-equipped Aero L-39 Albatros jet trainers painted white, red and blue.

The team then moved to Prerov airbase while construction and repair work was being carried out at Kosice, with their complement being increased to six aircraft for a performance at the local Moravian-Silesian Air Show.

When Czechoslovakia became the separate Czech Republic and Slovakia in 1993, the team became part of the new Slovakian Air Force. The following year, they began an international tour – performing in Denmark, the UK and Hungary with a seventh aircraft being added to the team for solo displays. The team was stripped back to five aircraft for the 2001 season before being disbanded in 2004.

the team during airshow season. The Patrulla Águila callsign is 'Aguila' and they are the only military team in Europe to use yellow smoke as part of their display. They are also said to be the only jet-flying team in the world who perform inverted loops – a challenging and uncomfortable manoeuvre that is only carried out by the team's most experienced solo pilot.

To date the team have performed at more than 300 airshows, clocking up more than 25,000 flying hours. While the C-101 was officially retired from its training role in the Spanish Air Force in August 2022, being replaced by the Pilatus PC-21 (E.27 in Spanish service), the Aviojet has been retained by the Patrulla Águila for the time being.

PATRULLA ASCUA, SPANISH AIR FORCE

During the years prior to the formation of Patrulla Águila, Spain had numerous different aerobatic teams. One of these was Patrulla Ascua or 'Ember Patrol', which was established without a name in 1956 and flew a quartet of F-86 Sabres.

Their first show took place shortly after their formation, on February 23, 1956, at Manises airbase but this was cut short by bad weather. Four months later, on June 22, 1956, they performed during the opening ceremony for the new airport in Rome, Italy. Although the F-86s were initially flown in their regular in-service colours, they would later receive an official Spanish flag-derived red and yellow paint job and the Patrulla Ascua name was applied in 1958. At this point, a fifth Sabre joined the team for solo demos. A crash on September 28, 1958, during a training flight led to the team's suspension for three years and despite a few more airshow appearances they were eventually wound up on January 12, 1965.

MODERN AEROBATIC TEAMS **039**

MODERN AEROBATIC TEAMS CHAPTER 1 – EUROPE

SWEDEN

040 MODERN AEROBATIC TEAMS

ACRO HUNTERS, SWEDISH AIR FORCE

The Swedish Air Force ordered 120 Hawker Hunter F.50s in 1954, with the type entering service the following year under the designation J 34. In 1956, the leader of F 18 Wing decided that an aerobatic team should be formed using the new aircraft to perform at the wing's 10th anniversary show.

This team, known at first as the Lampell-Group after its commander Sven Lampell, received four smoke dispenser-equipped J 34s and began training during March-April 1956. Their first public display was on June 1, 1956, and the team name was then changed to give a better indication of their purpose, i.e. aerial acrobatics in Hunters. Evidently regulations meant that since the Hunter was a foreign-made aircraft it could not appear at airshows outside Sweden, which was neutral – so the Acro Hunters only performed over home territory.

A fifth Hunter was added for solo work in 1957 and the last Acro Hunters display was at Malmslätt on September 1, 1962.

TEAM 60, SWEDISH AIR FORCE

The Hunters of the Acro Hunters were replaced with Saab J 35B Draken fighters and a new aerobatic team, the Acro Deltas, was formed in 1963. This lasted just three years, with the team being disbanded in 1966. A new Swedish Air Force team was then established in 1974 flying four Saab 105 aircraft – which were designated Sk 60 in Swedish service.

Like many others the new display team, known as Team 60 after the aircraft, was attached to a flight training institution, in this case the Air Force's Central Flying School at Ljungbyhed airbase in southern Sweden. Another Sk 60 was added in 1975 and the team's first public display took place at Gothenburg in May 1976.

While the aircraft were originally left in their standard camouflage colour scheme, they were equipped with white smoke generators. In later years a scheme based on Sweden's national colours of blue and yellow was applied and smoke pods were fitted in the underwing positions.

The team was temporarily disbanded in 2008 due to financial problems faced by the Swedish Air Force but was reinstated during 2018. Their last show was on June 22, 2024, with the Sk 60 finally being retired a week later.

▼ HAWKER HUNTER MK.50 (J 34)

Hawker Hunter MK.50 (J 34), E/9, Acro Hunters, F18 Wing, Svenska flygvapnet (Swedish Air Force), Tullinge airbase, Sweden, 1962.
Besides the team name painted on the nose, these Hunters had no visible differences from others serving in Sweden.

▼ SAAB 105

Saab 105, 125, Team 60, Flygskolan, Svenska flygvapnet (Royal Swedish Airschool, Swedish Air Force), Malmen airbase, Sweden, 2007.
The team's name was derived form the Swedish Air Force designation of the Saab 105 (Sk 60).

MODERN AEROBATIC TEAMS

MODERN AEROBATIC TEAMS CHAPTER 1 – EUROPE
SWITZERLAND

▼ HAWKER HUNTER MK.58
Hawker Hunter MK.58, J-4025/30, Patrouille Suisse, Schweizer Luftwaffe/Forces Aériennes Suisses/Forze Aeree Svizzere (Swiss Patrol, Swiss Air Force), Emmen Airbase, Lucerne, Switzerland, 1994. 1994 marked the 30th anniversary of the team but also their last year flying the Hunter.

▼ NORTHROP F-5E TIGER II
Northrop F-5E Tiger II, J-3088, Patrouille Suisse, Schweizer Luftwaffe/Forces Aériennes Suisses/Forze Aeree Svizzere (Swiss Patrol, Swiss Air Force), Emmen Airbase, Lucerne, Switzerland, 2022. Patrouille Suisse replaced the Hunter with the F-5 in 1994 and still flies that aircraft.

▼ PILATUS PC-7
Pilatus PC-7, A-916, PC-7 Team, A-916, Schweizer Luftwaffe/Forces Aériennes Suisses/Forze Aeree Svizzere (Swiss Air Force), Dübendorf Airbase, Lucerne, Switzerland, 2014 Switzerland.
The Swiss Air Force formally established a new team in 1989 using the locally-designed Pilatus PC-7 turboprop aircraft.

PATROUILLE SUISSE, SWISS AIR FORCE

Founded on August 22, 1964, Switzerland's Patrouille Suisse rank among the world's most famous and well-respected teams today. They initially flew four Hawker Hunters, with Dassault Mirage IIISs being flown by the team for just two displays during 1968. A fifth Hunter was added to the team in 1970, then a sixth, and smoke generators were fitted for the 1977 season. The team would continue to fly their Hunters for 30 years, finally replacing them with Northrop F-5E Tiger IIs in 1994. These were then fitted with smoke generators in 1996. The team maintains a total of 12 F-5Es in team colours but only six are used during displays.

Incredibly, the F-5Es have now also been operated by the Patrouille Suisse for 30 years – matching the Hunters. In 2014, plans were unveiled for a transition to the F/A-18C by the end of 2016, but this never came to pass. The Swiss Air Force now says that it intends for the Patrouille Suisse to continue flying the F-5E until the end of 2027, with the first Lockheed Martin F-35A Lightning II due to enter Swiss service in 2028.

Over the years, Patrouille Suisse have performed at hundreds of airshows. Currently, the team is supported by a Patrouille Suisse-liveried Pilatus PC-6 Porter utility aircraft named Felix, which transports their commander and announcer.

PC-7 TEAM, SWISS AIR FORCE

When the Swiss-made Pilatus PC-7 Turbo Trainer, a turboprop-powered tandem-seater, was introduced in 1982 the Swiss Air Force began using it for solo demonstrations. A full display team made up of nine volunteer pilots was then established in 1987. The name PC-7 Team was applied in 1989, as the air force celebrated its 75th anniversary, and the team was made permanent.

Ever since then, PC-7 Team have made several performances annually, even venturing abroad on rare occasions. PC-7 Team switched to flying nine upgraded NCPC-7s in October 2006 and smoke generators were eventually installed in 2014.

The team's pilots are all full-time military personnel and their 'day job' is flying F/A-18 fighters. While the team are stationed at Dübendorf Airbase they often operate from Militärflugplatz Emmen or Locarno Airport instead.

MODERN AEROBATIC TEAMS **043**

MODERN AEROBATIC TEAMS — CHAPTER 1 – EUROPE

TURKEY

▼ REPUBLIC F-84G THUNDERJET
Republic F-84G Thunderjet, 282, Mili, Türk Hava Kuvvetleri (National, Turkish Air Force), Balikesir airbase, Turkey, 1958.
The Mili was the first aerobatic team created in the THK in 1952.

▼ NORTH AMERICAN F-86E
North American F-86E, Uçan Kuğular, Türk Hava Kuvvetleri (Flying Swans, Turkish Air Force), Eskişehir airbase, Turkey, 1962.
The 'Flying Swans' flew in formations of nine to 12 aircraft during the 1960s; the aircraft has the previous THK roundel.

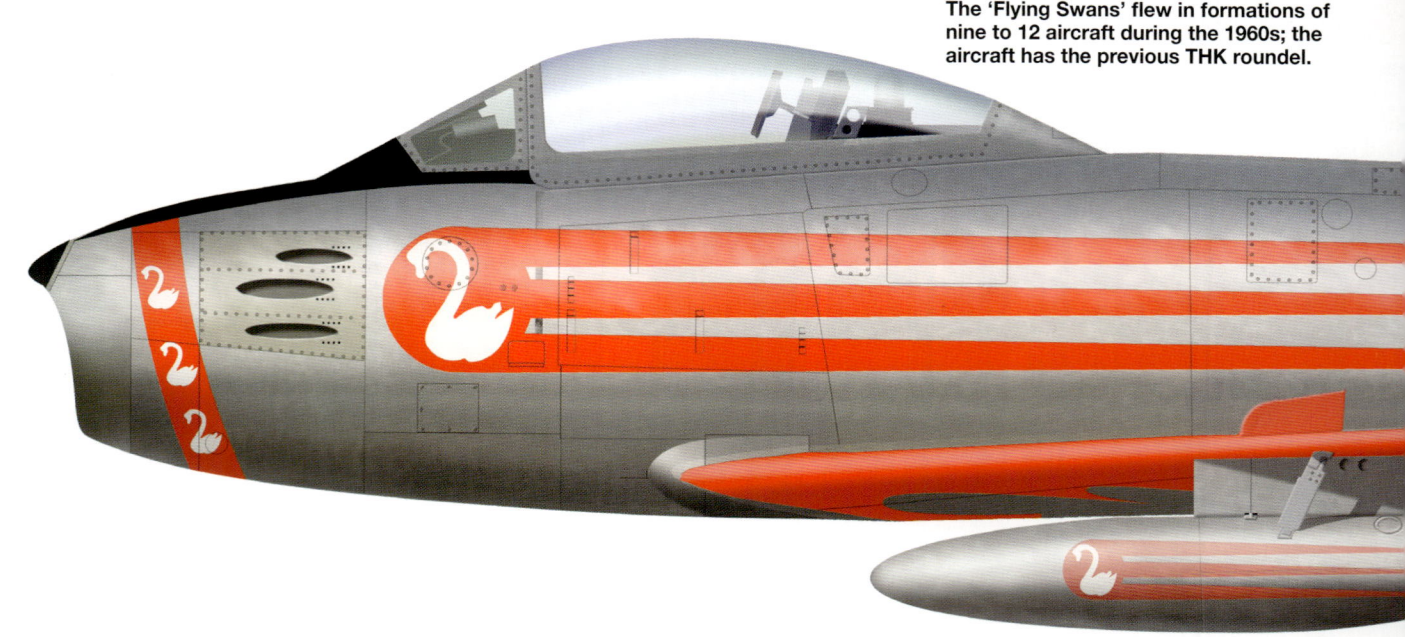

MILI, TURKISH AIR FORCE

Turkey operated the largest fleet of F-84s anywhere in the world – after the USA – with a total of 479 F-84Gs being delivered between 1952 and 1956. It was natural, then, that the first Turkish aerobatic team flew F-84Gs from its inception in 1952. The Mili team (Mili meaning 'National') was part of the 9th Airbase Command at Balikesir and continued to give demonstrations until 1962. While most displays were staged in Turkey, the team did also perform in Belgium and Italy.

UCAN KUGULAR, TURKISH AIR FORCE

A second team was formed by the Turkish Air Force in 1955 to showcase the skills of pilots flying F-86E Sabres. Like Mili, this team, dubbed Ucan Kugular or 'Flying Swans', operated for a decade – up to 1965. The team had 12 bare metal Sabres painted with red and white graphics, including several swan silhouette logos, and flew in formations of either nine or 12. Unlike Mili, Ucan Kugular never performed abroad.

MODERN AEROBATIC TEAMS

MODERN AEROBATIC TEAMS — CHAPTER 1 – EUROPE

▼ REPUBLIC F-84G THUNDERJET
Republic F-84G Thunderjet, 51-10703/703, Akrep, Türk Hava Kuvvetleri (Scorpion, Turkish Air Force), Diyarbakir airbase, Turkey, 1958.
This team performed for only two years before being disbanded in 1959.

▼ CANADAIR NF-5A
Canadair NF-5A, 7, Türk Yıldızları, Türk Hava Kuvvetleri (Turkish Stars, Turkish Air Force), Konya airbase, Turkey, 2023. The current display team of the Turkish Air Force have 10 NF-5As and two dual-seat NF-5Bs, although they usually use only eight aircraft in each display.

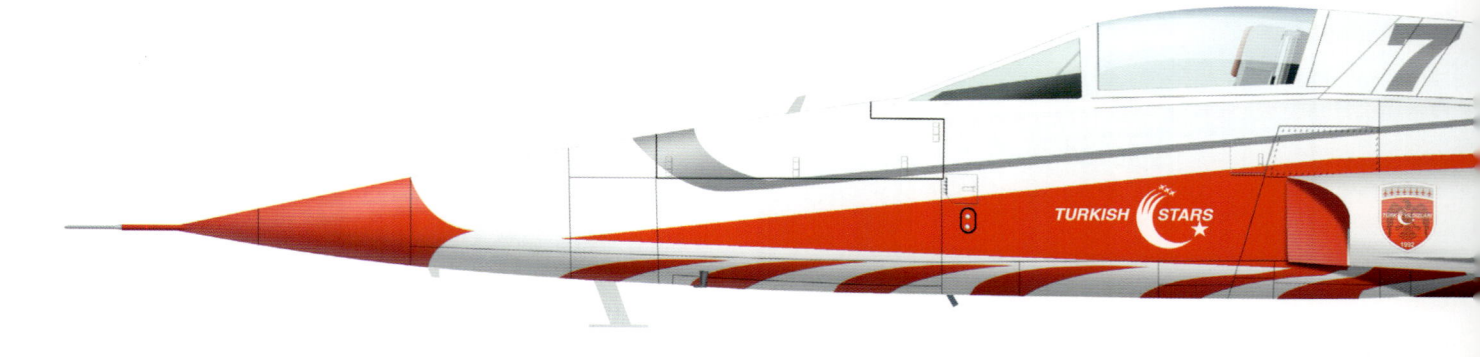

AKREP, TURKISH AIR FORCE

Mili and Ucan Kugular were joined by a third team in 1957: Akrep or 'Scorpions'. Perhaps unsurprisingly given the sheer quantity of the type in service, they were also equipped with F-84Gs. Located at the 8th Airbase Command in Diyarbekir, the team performed in both Turkey and Pakistan prior to their dissolution in 1959.

TURKISH STARS, TURKISH AIR FORCE

A new and unnamed Turkish Air Force display team was formed on November 7, 1992, from the 132nd Squadron stationed at the 3rd Main Jet Base Group Command in Konya. Just over two months later the team, equipped with seven Canadair NF-5s obtained from the Royal Netherlands Air Force, was given the name Turkish Stars. Their first demonstration flight was in 1994 at Diyarbekir.

By 2001, the team's formation had been expanded to encompass eight aircraft. This was then reduced back to seven – though the full team complement is actually 12. A new world record was set that year, on August 24, when the Turkish Stars performed in front of more than a million people at Baku in Azerbaijan.

Plans have evidently been drawn up to replace the team's NF-5s with locally-made TAI Hurjet advanced jet trainers over the next few years.

MODERN AEROBATIC TEAMS **047**

MODERN AEROBATIC TEAMS CHAPTER 1 – EUROPE

UNITED KINGDOM

▼ HAWKER HUNTER F.6

Hawker Hunter F.6, XF430, Black Arrows, 111 Squadron, Royal Air Force, RAF Wattisham, United Kingdom, 1959.
In 1958, the Black Arrows accomplished a world record loop manoeuvre using 22 aircraft.

BLACK ARROWS, RAF

The RAF's 111 Squadron, equipped with Gloster Meteor F.8s, formed an unofficial display team in 1955. The following year, re-equipped with Hawker Hunters, the team was solidified as the Black Arrows. In 1958, they would make history by executing a loop with 22 Hunters in formation at the Society of British Aircraft Constructors' show at Farnborough. It is a world record that has yet to be broken. Afterwards, they performed the world's first 16-aircraft barrel roll.

The core team consisted of just five aircraft, however, and this was expanded to nine later that year. The team was disbanded in 1960.

BLUE DIAMONDS, RAF

Following the dissolution of the Black Arrows, several ex-team members left 111 Squadron and subsequently joined another Hunter unit, 92 Squadron, where a new unnamed team was then brought into being. Training began towards the end of 1960 and in mid-January 1961 the squadron were posted to Cyprus where the good weather conditions allowed training to continue.

At the same time, the squadron's Hunters were given a royal blue paint scheme with a white flash along the fuselage. Returning from Cyprus in March 1961, the team were given approval to fly as an aerobatic nine. Efforts were made to find the team a name, with suggestions ranging from the Falcons to the Flying Cobras but in the end it was the German press who called them 'Die Blauen Diamanten' and that name stuck. In October 1961 the Blue Diamonds went on tour, displaying in Greece and Iran. After months of gunnery training during early 1962, the team continued formation flight training in July and a 16-strong Blue Diamonds formation then flew at that year's Farnborough Air Show. The team was retired at the beginning of 1963 as the squadron transitioned to fly English Electric Lightnings.

▼ HAWKER HUNTER F.6

Hawker Hunter F.6, XG189, Blue Diamonds, No. 92 Squadron, Royal Air Force, RAF Linton-on-Ouse, United Kingdom, 1962.
The Blue Diamonds performed using 16-aircraft formations.

MODERN AEROBATIC TEAMS **049**

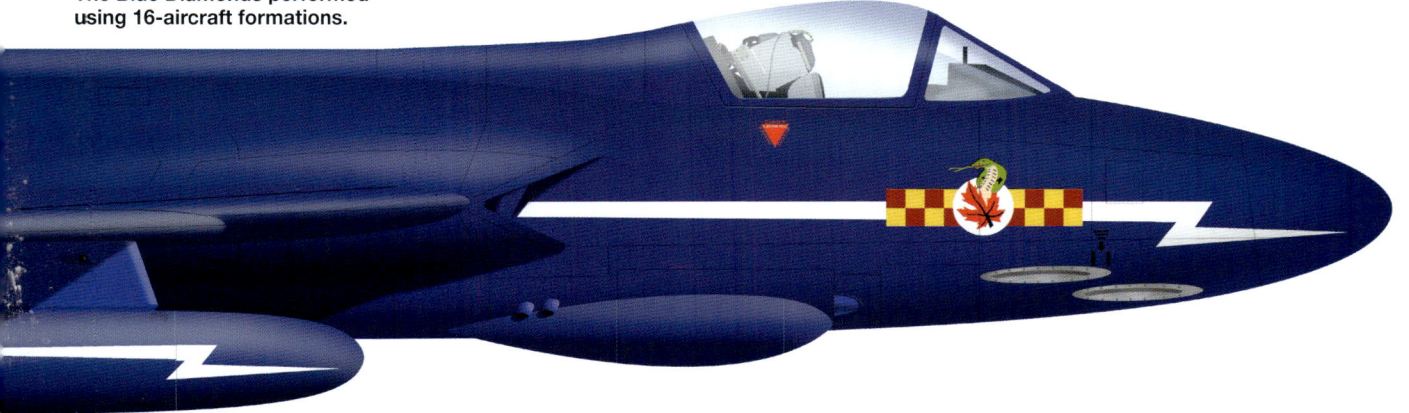

MODERN AEROBATIC TEAMS — CHAPTER 1 – EUROPE

▼ HUNTING JET PROVOST T.4

Hunting Jet Provost T.4, XN459, Red Pelicans, No. 2 Flying Training School, Royal Air Force, RAF Kemble, United Kingdom, 1962. Formed in 1958, the team would go through several name changes before settling on the Red Pelicans in 1963; in 1964 it would become the official RAF display team.

RED PELICANS, RAF

The RAF Central Flying School at RAF Little Rissington had flown piston-engined Hunting Percival Provosts up to the mid-1950s when these were replaced with new Jet Provost T.1 trainers. In 1958 the school's four-ship display team, the Sparrows, also switched to the Jet Provost. By the following year, the Sparrows had become a duo known as the Redskins and the school began to receive new Jet Provost T.3s to replace its T.1s. The Redskins were disbanded and a new four-ship team, the Pelicans, was set up instead. Halfway through the 1962 season, the Pelicans were reequipped with T.4s and these were fitted with a smoke system. Two more T.4s were added for the 1963 season and the six aircraft were painted in Day-Glo red – prompting the team to change their name, naturally enough, to the Red Pelicans. Displays in France and Belgium, as well as across the UK, followed and at the end of 1963 it was decided that they should become the official aerobatic team of the RAF.

During 1965, with the Folland Gnat now in service, the Red Pelicans became second fiddle to the new Red Arrows team and were stripped back to just four aircraft again – and without smoke generators this time. More shows continued into the 1970s, with the team having been reequipped with T.5s in 1970, before disbandment at the end of the 1973 season.

▼ BAC LIGHTNING F.1A

BAC Lightning F.1A, XM177/G, Firebirds, No. 56 Squadron, Royal Air Force, RAF Wattisham, United Kingdom, 1963.
The Firebirds were the last RAF aerobatic team to use fighter aircraft.

MODERN AEROBATIC TEAMS **051**

MODERN AEROBATIC TEAMS   CHAPTER 1 – EUROPE

▼ HUNTING JET PROVOST T.4
Hunting Jet Provost T.4, XP629, The Macaws, College of Air Warfare, Royal Air Force, RAF Manby, United Kingdom, 1968.
Initially knows as the Magistrates, the team was renamed the Macaws in 1967 and had this as its initial colour scheme.

▼ HUNTING JET PROVOST T.4
Hunting Jet Provost T.4, XP563/78, Cranwell Poachers, Royal Air Force College, Royal Air Force, RAF Cranwell, United Kingdom, 1970.
Formed at the RAF College, the team initially went by the name Cranwell Poachers from 1969 until 1971; they then flew as the Poachers until their disbandment in 1976.

FIREBIRDS, RAF

From 1962 to 1963, the official aerobatic team of the RAF was the Tigers from 74 Squadron – equipped with nine English Electric Lightning F.1A aircraft. This made them the first team in the world to fly aircraft capable of reaching Mach 2. From 1963, the mantle of 'official team' was inherited by 56 Squadron, who had established their own team comprising nine Lightnings, known as the Firebirds, the year before.

The team's first show was at Waterbeach, Cambridgeshire, on May 24 with the second on June 3 at North Weald in Essex. Three days later, two of the aircraft were involved in a collision over Wattisham and one pilot was seriously injured when his ejection seat failed to operate correctly. The team took 13 aircraft with them to Le Bourget on June 12 to participate in the 25th Paris Air Salon and on June 16 performed a nine-ship loop – arguably the high point of their career.

The Firebirds were disbanded in 1964, becoming the last official RAF team to fly front line fighters.

THE MACAWS, RAF

Another Jet Provost T.4 aerobatic team, besides the Red Pelicans, was formed at the RAF's College of Air Warfare in Manby, Lincolnshire, in 1965. Known as the Magistrates, their aircraft wore a standard silver-orange colour scheme.

At the conclusion of the 1967 season, the team were renamed as the Macaws – this being a variety of parrot as well as a clever acronym derived from MAnby College of Air Warfare. The team's Jet Provosts were given a new red and grey paint scheme for 1968 and the following year this was

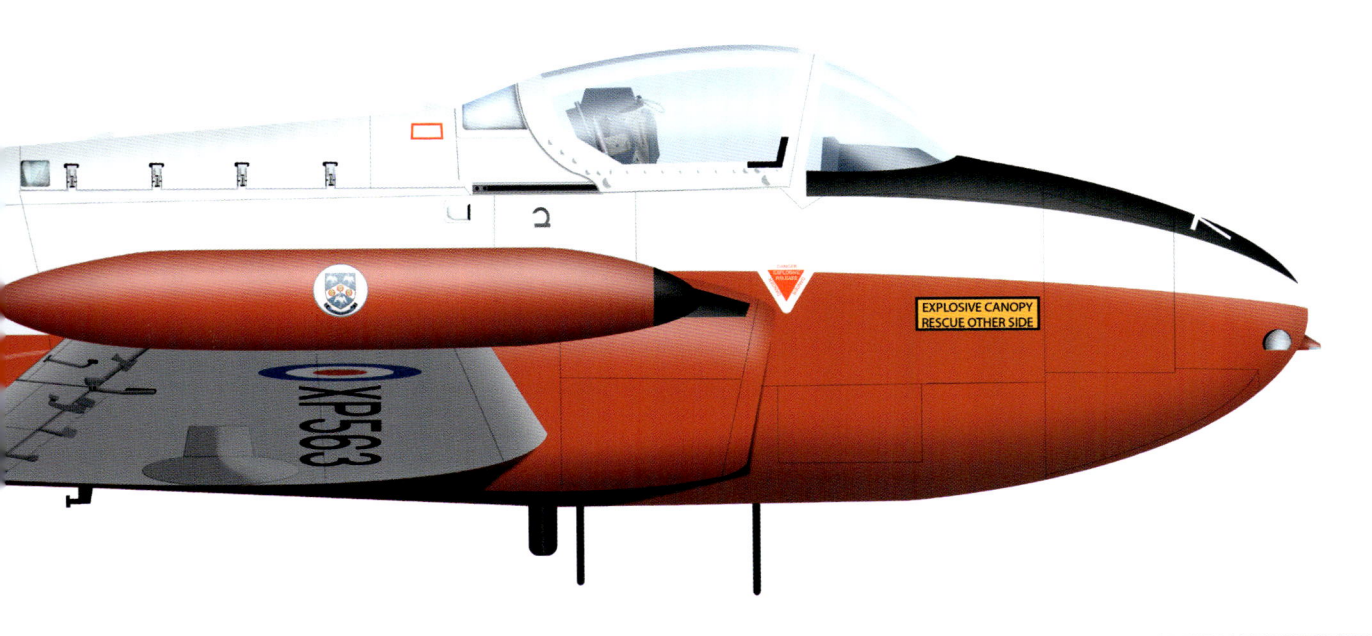

MODERN AEROBATIC TEAMS **053**

MODERN AEROBATIC TEAMS CHAPTER 1 – EUROPE

▼ **BAE HAWK T.1**
BAe Hawk T.1, XX308, Red Arrows, Royal Air Force, RAF Scampton, United Kingdom, 1985. The Hawk entered service with the team in 1979.

054 MODERN AEROBATIC TEAMS

replaced with a red, grey and white scheme plus a parrot logo on the nose. After performances at shows across Europe, including in Germany and France, the team were disbanded in 1973.

CRANWELL POACHERS, RAF

Yet another four-ship Jet Provost T.4 team was formed at RAF College Cranwell in 1969 – this time called the Cranwell Poachers. After a couple of years, the somewhat superfluous 'Cranwell' was dropped from the name and the team became simply the Poachers. At the same time they were reequipped with T.5s. However, Britain's economy began to struggle as the 1970s wore on and in 1976 the Poachers were disbanded to save money. They had, by that time, become the last of the Jet Provost-equipped RAF aerobatic teams.

RED ARROWS, RAF

The two-seater Folland Gnat T.1 jet trainer entered service at the No. 4 Flying Training School at RAF Valley in November 1962 and during the summer of 1963 a new Gnat aerobatic team was established, informally, by the school's flying instructors. During early 1964 they took their name, and livery, from the callsign of their leader, ex-Black Arrows member Flight Lieutenant Lee Jones: Yellowjack. The five Yellowjacks aircraft were painted in bright yellow and equipped with white smoke generators. The team then showcased the aircraft's qualities at the Farnborough Air Show in September 1964.

While it was clear that the tiny Gnat was an excellent aircraft for aerobatics, the RAF felt that the team name and bright yellow paintwork were less than ideal. Therefore, in November 1964, the team was re-formed under the new name Red Arrows – with seven Gnats painted in bright red – as the new official RAF aerobatic display team. Jones remained the leader and the team's first display was during a press day on May

▼ FOLLAND GNAT T.1
Folland Gnat T.1, XR986, Red Arrows, Royal Air Force, RAF Kemble, United Kingdom, 1971.
The Red Arrows were formed in 1965 and their first aircraft was the Gnat.

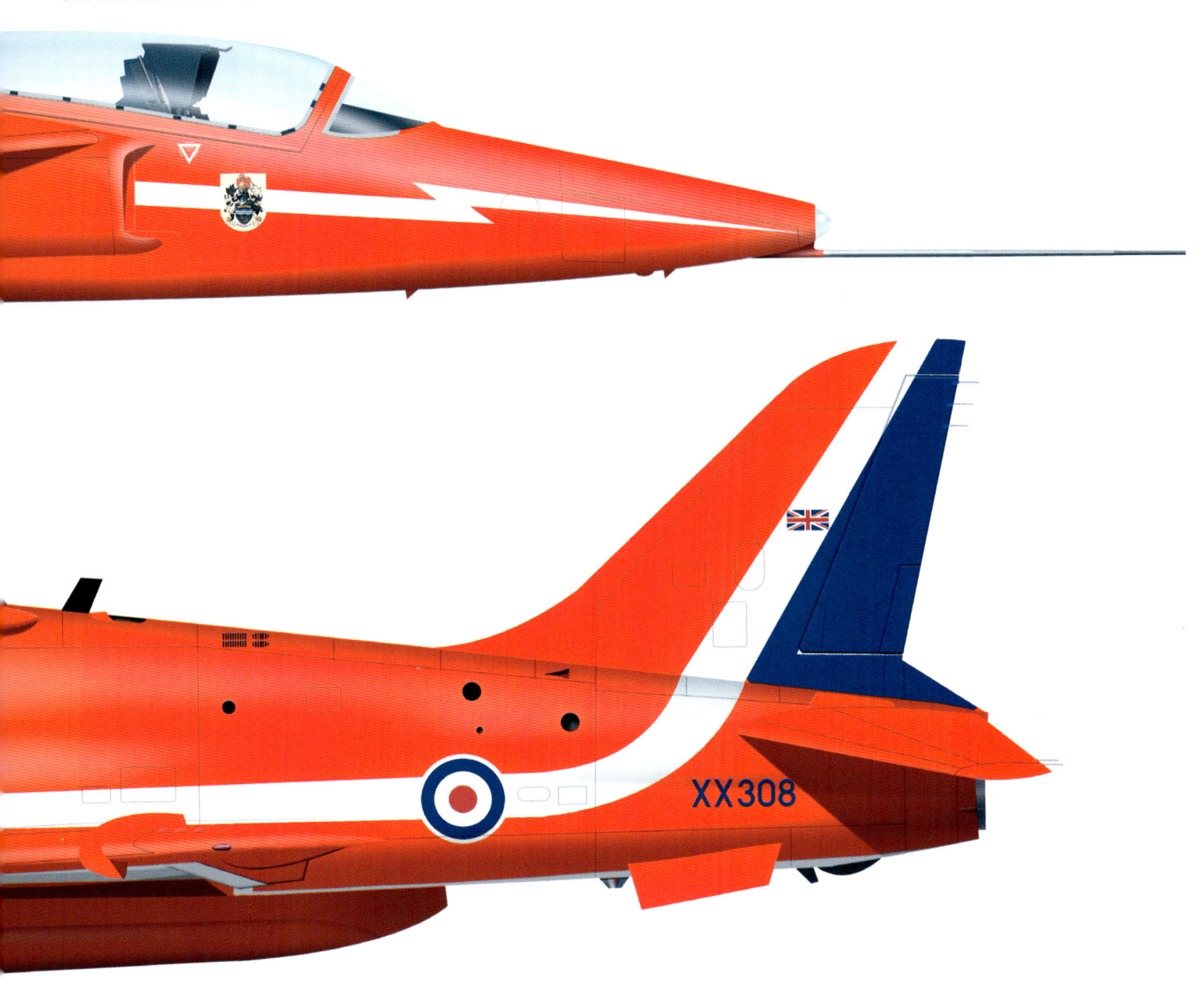

MODERN AEROBATIC TEAMS — CHAPTER 1 – EUROPE

▼ **BAE HAWK T.1**

BAe Hawk T.1, XX325, Red Arrows, Royal Air Force, RAF Scampton, United Kingdom, 2014. This aircraft displays the special markings of the 50th anniversary of the team.

6, 1965, at Little Rissington. By the end of their first season, they had clocked up an astonishing 65 displays across Britain, Belgium, France, Germany, Italy and the Netherlands.

When Jones's time as Red Leader ended, he was replaced by former Red 3 Ray Hanna – who held the position for a record four years and oversaw the expansion of the team to nine Gnats in 1966, thereby making a diamond-nine formation possible. The team flew 1,292 displays using the Gnat before transitioning to the new British Aerospace Hawk T.1 jet trainer in 1979 – the aircraft that the present-day iteration of the team continue to fly today.

Currently based at RAF Waddington, the team's nine pilots (no spare) are all volunteers and must have completed one or more operational tours on a fast jet, have accumulated at least 1,500 flying hours and been assessed as above average in their operational role. More than 90 people work with the team in engineering and support roles and they are known collectively as The Blues.

The history of the Red Arrows could fill this entire volume but suffice to say that they have flown thousands of shows over the decades and still fly Hawk T.1 jet trainers today.

ROUGH DIAMONDS, ROYAL NAVY

Not to be outdone by the RAF, the Royal Navy's Fleet Air Arm had numerous aerobatic display teams of its own. One of these, the Rough Diamonds, was formed from 738 Squadron at Brawdy airbase during the summer of 1965. They flew a quartet of Hawker Hunter GA.11 aircraft in standard RN colours – except for that of the leader, Lieutenant Commander Christopher Comins, whose Hunter had a Day-Glo red nose and wingtips. The team was disbanded in 1969.

▼ HAWKER HUNTER GA.11

Hawker Hunter GA.11, XF287/781/BY, The Rough Diamonds, 738 Naval Air Squadron, Fleet Air Arm, Royal Navy, RNAS Lossiemouth, United Kingdom, 1966.
This team used Hunters in regular FAA colours, with the exception of the commander's aircraft which had the nose, spine and wing tips in Day-Glo.

MODERN AEROBATIC TEAMS **057**

MODERN AEROBATIC TEAMS — CHAPTER 1 – EUROPE

YUGOSLAVIA

▼ CANADAIR CL-13 MK.4
Canadair CL-13 MK.4, 11120, akro grupa 204, Ratno vazduhoplovstvo i protivvazdušna odbrana (Acro Group 204, Yugoslavian Air Force), Batajnica Airbase, Yugoslavia, 1960.
This was the first jet aircraft display team of the Yugoslavian Air Force; it performed from 1959 until 1964.

ACRO GROUP 204, YUGOSLAVIAN AIR FORCE
Existing from 1918 to 1992, Yugoslavia comprised six republics – Bosnia and Herzegovina, Croatia, Macedonia, Montenegro, Serbia and Slovenia – all of which are separate countries today. The Yugoslavian Air Force's first jet display team was formed from the 204th Fighter Aviation Regiment at Batajnica airbase in 1959 flying four yellow and blue Canadair CL-13 Mk.4 Sabres.
Their first public performance was in front of the president of Sudan and 80,000 spectators during an official visit to Leskovac, Serbia, in July 1960. Further shows followed, with the team expanding

▼ SOKO G-2 GALEB
Soko G-2 Galeb, 23167, Vazduhoplovna vojna akademija, Ratno vazduhoplovstvo i protivvazdušna odbrana (Air Force Academy, Yugoslavian Air Force), Zemunik Airbase, Yugoslavia, 1970.
The Yugoslav air force had several aerobatic teams using locally designed aircraft and one of those was created at the academy using the Soko G-2 trainer. This aircraft displays the special colour scheme created for the team as, at first, they flew in standard camouflage.

UKRAINE

▼ MIKOYAN MIG-29A
Mikoyan MiG-29A, 103, Ukrayins'ki Sokoly, Povitriyani syly Zbroiynyh syl Ukraiyini (Ukrainian Falcons, Ukrainian Air Force), Kirovske airbase, Ukraine, 1997.
Although several displays were made before, it was in 1996 that the Ukrainian Falcons combined the MiG-29 aircraft and its new name into a new formation.

UKRAINIAN FALCONS, UKRAINIAN AIR FORCE
Shortly after the break-up of the Soviet Union, a MiG-29-equipped duo was formed in the newly independent Ukraine as the UkrAF MiG-29 Demonstration Team. This small team gave performances at several international airshows in 1992 under the title The Ukrainian Tridents Tour.

to five Sabres before being disbanded in 1964.

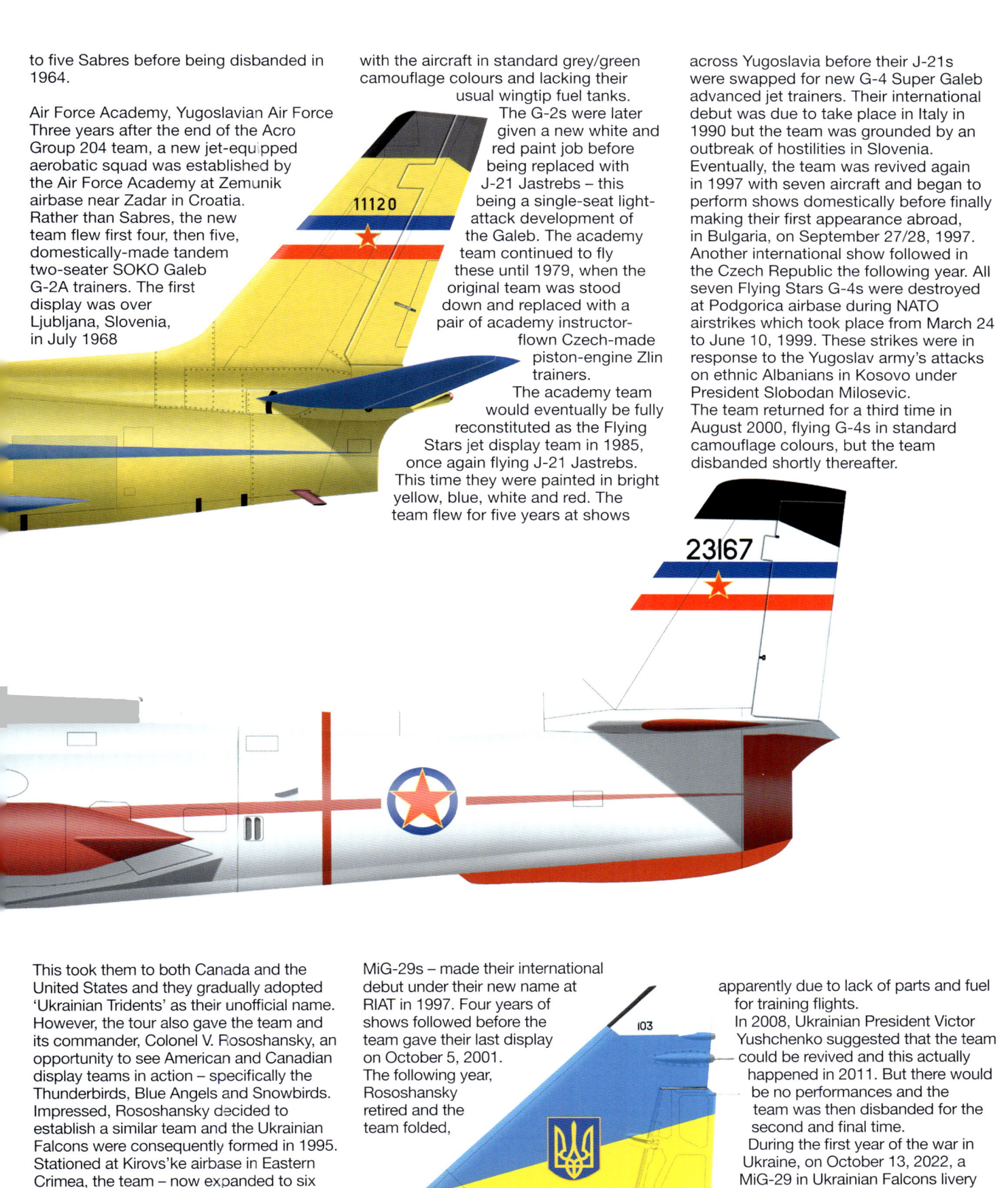

Air Force Academy, Yugoslavian Air Force

Three years after the end of the Acro Group 204 team, a new jet-equipped aerobatic squad was established by the Air Force Academy at Zemunik airbase near Zadar in Croatia. Rather than Sabres, the new team flew first four, then five, domestically-made tandem two-seater SOKO Galeb G-2A trainers. The first display was over Ljubljana, Slovenia, in July 1968 with the aircraft in standard grey/green camouflage colours and lacking their usual wingtip fuel tanks.

The G-2s were later given a new white and red paint job before being replaced with J-21 Jastrebs – this being a single-seat light-attack development of the Galeb. The academy team continued to fly these until 1979, when the original team was stood down and replaced with a pair of academy instructor-flown Czech-made piston-engine Zlin trainers.

The academy team would eventually be fully reconstituted as the Flying Stars jet display team in 1985, once again flying J-21 Jastrebs. This time they were painted in bright yellow, blue, white and red. The team flew for five years at shows across Yugoslavia before their J-21s were swapped for new G-4 Super Galeb advanced jet trainers. Their international debut was due to take place in Italy in 1990 but the team was grounded by an outbreak of hostilities in Slovenia. Eventually, the team was revived again in 1997 with seven aircraft and began to perform shows domestically before finally making their first appearance abroad, in Bulgaria, on September 27/28, 1997. Another international show followed in the Czech Republic the following year. All seven Flying Stars G-4s were destroyed at Podgorica airbase during NATO airstrikes which took place from March 24 to June 10, 1999. These strikes were in response to the Yugoslav army's attacks on ethnic Albanians in Kosovo under President Slobodan Milosevic.

The team returned for a third time in August 2000, flying G-4s in standard camouflage colours, but the team disbanded shortly thereafter.

This took them to both Canada and the United States and they gradually adopted 'Ukrainian Tridents' as their unofficial name. However, the tour also gave the team and its commander, Colonel V. Rososhansky, an opportunity to see American and Canadian display teams in action – specifically the Thunderbirds, Blue Angels and Snowbirds. Impressed, Rososhansky decided to establish a similar team and the Ukrainian Falcons were consequently formed in 1995. Stationed at Kirovs'ke airbase in Eastern Crimea, the team – now expanded to six MiG-29s – made their international debut under their new name at RIAT in 1997. Four years of shows followed before the team gave their last display on October 5, 2001. The following year, Rososhansky retired and the team folded, apparently due to lack of parts and fuel for training flights.

In 2008, Ukrainian President Victor Yushchenko suggested that the team could be revived and this actually happened in 2011. But there would be no performances and the team was then disbanded for the second and final time.

During the first year of the war in Ukraine, on October 13, 2022, a MiG-29 in Ukrainian Falcons livery was destroyed during a combat mission in Vinnytsia Oblast after the pilot ejected having shot down a number of Russian-launched Iranian Shahed 136 drones.

MODERN AEROBATIC TEAMS **059**

CHAPTER 2 – NORTH AMERICA
CANADA

▼ CANADAIR CL-13 MK.2 SABRE
Canadair CL-13 MK.2 Sabre, 19415, Fireballs, 1st Air Division, Royal Canadian Air Force, Zweibrucken airbase, Germany, 1954.
The Fireballs performed in Europe, their pilots and aircraft being drawn from several squadrons of the 1st Air Division.

▼ CANADAIR MK.5 SABRE
Canadair MK.5 Sabre, 23066, Golden Hawks demonstration team, Royal Canadian Air Force, Chatam airbase, New Brunswick, Canada, 1962.
The team displayed their golden aircraft from 1959 until 1964.

FIREBALLS, ROYAL CANADIAN AIR FORCE

Alongside another team called the Sky Lancers, the Fireballs were the official aerobatic team of Canada's No. 1 Air Division in Europe between 1954 and 1956 – flying all-red F-86 Sabres. However, the team were disbanded, alongside the Sky Lancers, in 1956 after four of the five Sky Lancers pilots were killed during a training flight. The RCAF then suspended all aerobatics for two years.

GOLDEN HAWKS, ROYAL CANADIAN AIR FORCE

A request to create a new aerobatic team was submitted to RCAF command in 1958 on the basis that this would form part of the celebrations for the air force's 35th anniversary the following year. The request was approved for one year initially and a six-aircraft team with eight pilots was officially formed on March 1, 1959. The aircraft in question was the Canadair F-86 Sabre Mk.5 – the latest variant and Canada's front-line fighter – and all six were given a metallic gold paint scheme.

The team, led by Squadron Leader Fern Villeneuve, were given three months to get ready for a pre-planned summer season of performances. Evidently, in spite of what had happened to the Sky Lancers, the Golden Hawks quickly earned a reputation for their high-risk manoeuvres – flying at 50ft altitude for solo passes and 100ft for formation flypasts. Two pilots were killed during initial training but there were no serious incidents during their actual performances.

The Golden Hawks proved so popular that they earned a stay of execution, being re-established for a 1960 season. Eventually, they went on to fly a total of five seasons totalling 317 shows across North America. They were finally disbanded, on February 7, 1964, for financial reasons.

MODERN AEROBATIC TEAMS **061**

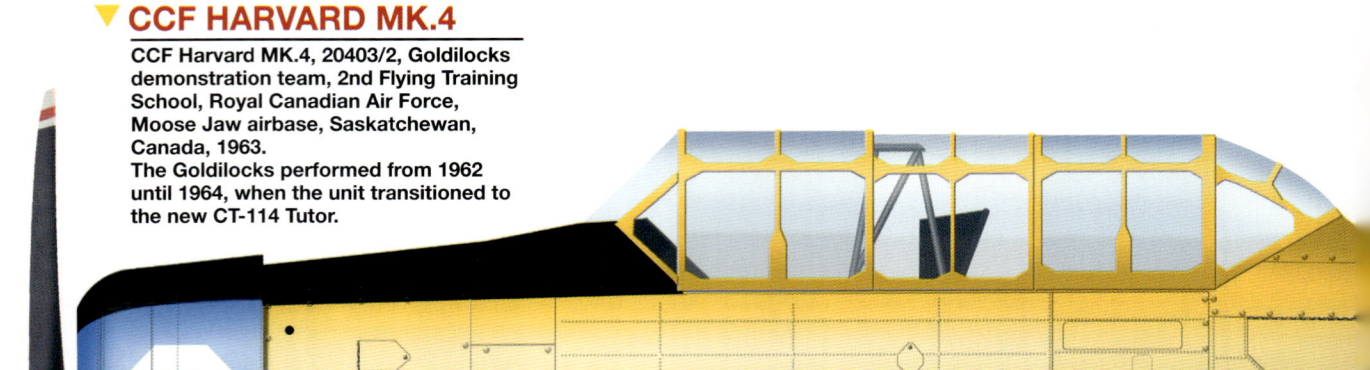

MODERN AEROBATIC TEAMS — CHAPTER 2 – NORTH AMERICA

▼ CCF HARVARD MK.4
CCF Harvard MK.4, 20403/2, Goldilocks demonstration team, 2nd Flying Training School, Royal Canadian Air Force, Moose Jaw airbase, Saskatchewan, Canada, 1963.
The Goldilocks performed from 1962 until 1964, when the unit transitioned to the new CT-114 Tutor.

▼ CANADAIR CT-114 TUTOR
CCF Harvard MK.4, 20403/2, Goldilocks demonstration team, 2nd Flying Training School, Royal Canadian Air Force, Moose Jaw airbase, Saskatchewan, Canada, 1963.
The Goldilocks performed from 1962 until 1964, when the unit transitioned to the new CT-114 Tutor.

062 MODERN AEROBATIC TEAMS

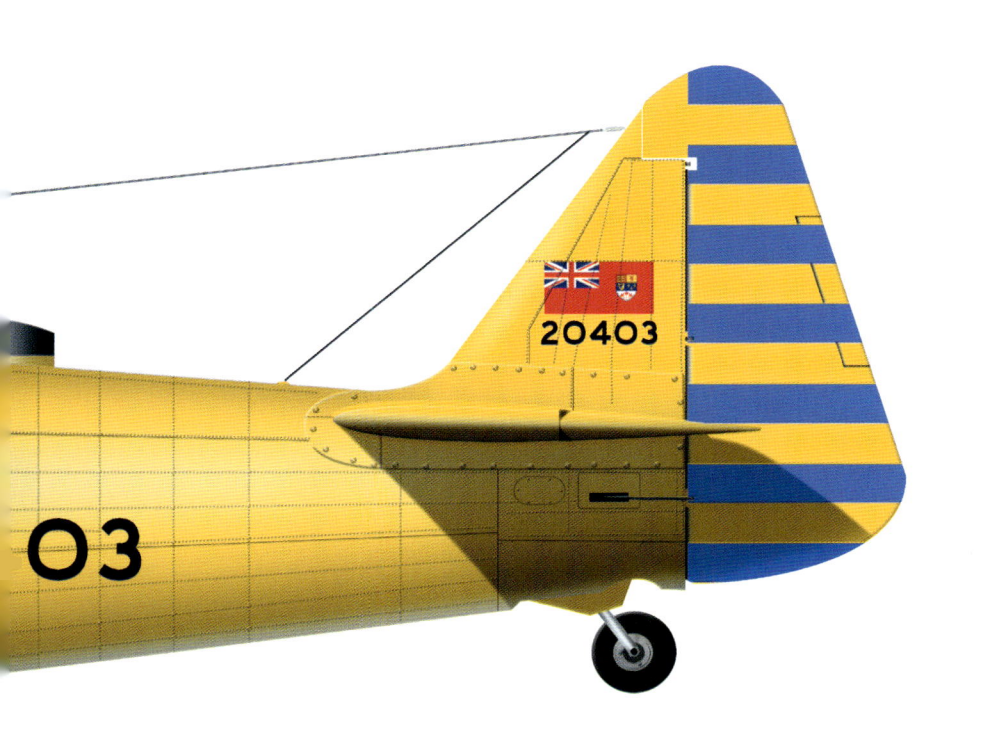

GOLDILOCKS, ROYAL CANADIAN AIR FORCE

Intended as a parody of the mighty Golden Hawks, the Goldilocks were formed at the Moose Jaw training base in 1962. Rather than flying Sabres fast jets, they flew old AT-16 Harvard Mk.4 piston engine trainers – painted bright yellow with blue or red accents. Pilot training switched to Canadair CT-114 Tutor jet trainers two years later and the Goldilocks team was disbanded.

GOLDEN CENTENNAIRES, ROYAL CANADIAN AIR FORCE

Three years after the Golden Hawks' disbandment, in 1967, a new aerobatic team was created to mark the 100th anniversary of the creation of Canada as a nation. The Golden Centennaires, as they were called, flew an odd mix of aircraft including nine gold and blue CT-114 Tutors in formation, a solo CF-101 Voodoo, a solo CF-104 Starfighter and two ancient Avro 504K biplanes. They also had two CT-133 Silver Star Support aircraft painted up in team colours and gave an impressive 103 displays in Canada plus seven more in the USA – all in 1967. The final show of their only season was in November that year at Nellis Air Force Base in Nevada.

MODERN AEROBATIC TEAMS

MODERN AEROBATIC TEAMS — CHAPTER 2 – NORTH AMERICA

▼ CANADAIR CT-114 TUTOR

Canadair CT-114 Tutor, 1, Snowbirds, 431 Air Demonstration Squadron/431e Escadron de Démonstration Aérienne, Royal Canadian Air Force/Aviation Royale Canadienne, Moose Jaw airbase, Saskatchewan, Canada, 1975. The Snowbirds had its origins in the former Golden Centenaries team; initially an informal team was created from the aircraft of the previous team, until, in 1974, it became the official demonstration team of the RCAF/ARC

▼ CANADAIR CT-114 TUTOR

Canadair CT-114 Tutor, 114051/2, Snowbirds, 431 Air Demonstration Squadron/431e Escadron de démonstration aérienne, Royal Canadian Air Force/Aviation Royale Canadienne, Moose Jaw airbase, Saskatchewan, Canada, 2023.
This aircraft is shown in the second and current colour scheme of the team.

064   MODERN AEROBATIC TEAMS

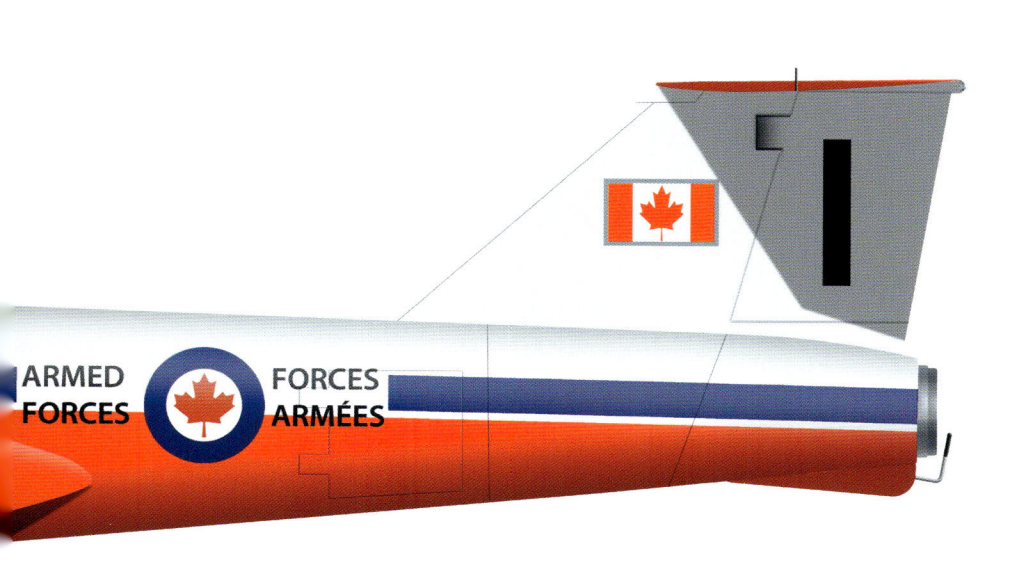

SNOWBIRDS, ROYAL CANADIAN AIR FORCE

The commander of Moose Jaw training base – and former commander of the Golden Centennaires – Colonel Owen Bartley Philp decided to form a new aerobatic team using ex-Centennaires CT-114s in 1969. The aircraft were still fitted out for display flying but had been given a coat of white anti-corrosion paint since the Centennaires were wound up. Eventually Philp got four Tutors flying together at the Abbotsford Air Show under the moniker 2 Canadian Forces Flying Training School Formation Team. Informally, the new team were known as the 'Tutor Whites'. By the following year, the team had 11 pilots and were flying seven aircraft. Formation flying transitioned to more complex manoeuvres and the team gradually gained official recognition.

'Tutor Whites' was not an especially inspired name, so the team held a competition at CFB Moose Jaw's Bushell Park Elementary School to come up with a better one. The result was Snowbirds – reflecting the white paint scheme and the team's Canadian origins. This was formally adopted on June 25, 1971. Four more years passed before the team was made the official Canadian Forces Air Demonstration Team, on January 15, 1978. Less than three months later, on April 1, 1978, the team was formed into its own unit: 431 Squadron, later to become 431 Air Demonstration Squadron.

Since then, the Snowbirds have continued to be the official aerobatics team of the Canadian Air Force, based at 15 Wing Moose Jaw, near Moose Jaw, Saskatchewan. The majority of CT-114s were retired in 2000, with the type having been replaced by the BAE Systems Hawk (CT-155 Hawk in Canadian service) and Beechcraft CT-156 Harvard IIs. However, the Snowbirds continue to operate 11 CT-114s today: nine plus two spares. A small number of additional machines are maintained in storage.

Around 80 personnel work with the squadron full time, 24 of whom travel as part of the team during show season. Apparently the Snowbirds were the first aerobatic team in the world to use music in their show, as well as live commentary from the pilots themselves while they are performing.

Tragedy struck in 2020 when a bird strike caused a 57-year-old Snowbirds CT-114 to crash shortly after take-off in Kamloops, British Columbia. While the pilot survived, the passenger, Captain Jennifer Casey, was killed when her ejection seat failed to function properly.

MODERN AEROBATIC TEAMS

MODERN AEROBATIC TEAMS CHAPTER 2 – NORTH AMERICA

USA

▼ LOCKHEED F-80B SHOOTING STAR
Lockheed F-80B Shooting Star, FT-481, Acrojets, USAF Fighter School, United States Air Force, Williams airbase, Arizona, USA, 1950.
The Acrojets were the first USAF aerobatic team flying jet aircraft.

▼ NORTH AMERICAN F-86F SABRE
North American F-86F Sabre, FU-464, Arctic Gladiators, 720th Fighter-Bomber Squadron, United States Air Force, Eielson Air Force Base, Alaska USA, 1954.
The Arctic Gladiators flew in standard colour scheme and performed only in Alaska; the team would be disbanded a year later in 1955.

▼ GRUMMAN F9F-8 COUGAR
Grumman F9F-8 Cougar, 131210/3, Blue Angels, United States Navy, NAS Pensacola, Florida, USA, 1956.
The Cougar was used by the team from 1955 until 1957; they had both the single and two-seat variants.

066 MODERN AEROBATIC TEAMS

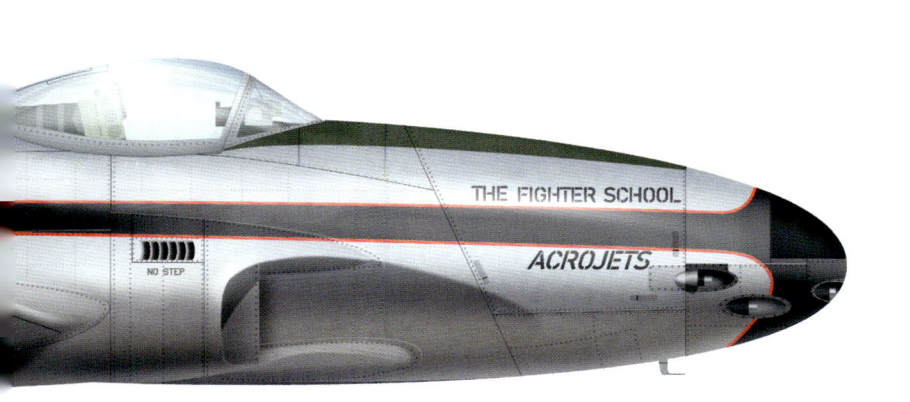

ACROJETS, USAF

The USAF's first official display team, and the first American team equipped with jets, was the Acrojets. They were formed in June 1948, nine months after the establishment of the air force as an independent branch of the United States Armed Forces, from instructors at the USAF Fighter School at Williams airbase, Arizona. Their first performance was at the school's graduation class that year flying four F-80A Shooting Stars. Official recognition came in March 1949. Evidently the team struggled to fly complex manoeuvres due to the unresponsive nature of the F-80's J33 engine. Acceleration was slow and if full throttle was applied abruptly the engine would simply stop. After a year of this, the team upgraded to the more powerful F-80C which alleviated these difficulties somewhat.

Most of the team were reassigned to operational units during the Korean War in 1951 and the team was disbanded – though a new version was later formed at Fürstenfeldbruck airbase, West Germany in 1955 by original Acrojets pilot Lieutenant Michael Smolen. This time they were equipped with T-33s and flew until 1957.

MODERN AEROBATIC TEAMS **067**

MODERN AEROBATIC TEAMS CHAPTER 2 – NORTH AMERICA

▼ MCDONNELL DOUGLAS F-4J PHANTOM II
McDonnell Douglas F-4J Phantom II, 153076/6, Blue Angels, US Navy, NAS Pensacola, Florida, 1970.
The Phantom was used by the Blue Angels from 1968 to 1973 before transitioning to the A-4 Skyhawk. The Phantoms carried dummy AIM-7 Sparrow air-to-air missiles.

▼ LOCKHEED C-130J HERCULES
Lockheed C-130J Hercules, 170000, Fat Albert, Blue Angels, United States Marines Corps, NAS Pensacola, Florida, 2020.
The Blue Angels received the new Fat Albert, an ex-RAF C-130J, in 2020.

ARCTIC GLADIATORS, USAF

When the USAF's 720th Fighter Bomber Squadron, equipped with F-86F Sabres, were reassigned to Eielson airbase in Alaska in June 1954 they very quickly formed a new demonstration team and called themselves the Arctic Gladiators. Their aircraft wore the squadron's standard silver and red paint scheme and their demonstrations only took place within the state of Alaska. Just over a year after their formation, on August 8, 1955, the 720th FBS were redesignated as the 455th FBS – and this resulted in the Arctic Gladiators' permanent dissolution.

BLUE ANGELS, US NAVY

After the Patrouille de France, the US Navy Flight Demonstration Squadron, aka the Blue Angels, is the oldest formal aerobatic team in the world.

They are also one of the world's busiest teams – performing at least 60 shows at 30 locations throughout the US (and two in Canada) every year. Since 1946, they have been seen by an estimated 505 million spectators.

Having been originally formed in April 1946 as the Navy Flight Exhibition Team, the Blue Angels got their more colourful name from an advert in the New Yorker magazine for a New York nightclub called The Blue Angel and were first introduced as such at a show in July 1946.

The team's first aircraft, Grumman F6F-5 Hellcats, were painted in dark navy blue with gold lettering. The still-current bright blue and yellow shades were adopted when they switched to the Grumman F8F-1 Bearcat in August 1946. Part of their routine was to fly mock dogfights against a yellow-painted North American SNJ-4 piston engine trainer dubbed the 'Beetle Bomb', which represented a Japanese Mitsubishi Zero.

Three years later, in 1949, the team switched to flying Grumman F9F-2B Panther jets. After a hiatus during the Korean War, the team re-formed and switched again, this time to F9F-6 Cougars. Having consisted of five aircraft up to this point, the team added a sixth aircraft in September 1956.

▼ MCDONNELL DOUGLAS/BOEING F/A-18E SUPER HORNET

McDonnell Douglas/Boeing F/A-18E Super Hornet, 165536/5, Blue Angels, United States Navy, NAS Pensacola, Florida, 2021.
The Super Hornet is the latest aircraft flown by the Blue Angels, flying since 2021.

MODERN AEROBATIC TEAMS CHAPTER 2 – NORTH AMERICA

▼ MCDONNELL FH-1 PHANTOM
McDonnell FH-1 Phantom, 111785, Marine Phantoms aerobatic team, United States Marines Corps, NAS Pensacola, Florida, 1949.
In early 1049, pilots from the VMF-122 squadron formed an aerobatic team, initially flying in standard colours, this new scheme was created later that year.

▼ LOCKHEED F-80B LIGHTNING
Lockheed F-80B Lightning, 45-8672, Minute Men Aerobatic Team, 120th Fighter-Interceptor Squadron, 140th Fighter-Interceptor Group, Colorado Air National Guard, Buckley Field, Colorado, 1956.
Elements of the Colorado ANG 120th Squadron constituted the ANG's official aerobatic team, the Minute Men; the F-80 was the first aircraft used.

The following year, following a now familiar pattern, the Blue Angels transitioned to the supersonic F11F-1 Tiger. This type was retained for longer than its predecessors and the team flew it during a tour of Caribbean islands and Europe in 1965.

The team finally swapped their Tigers for McDonnell Douglas F-4J Phantom IIs in 1969, the pilots nearly always flying with the back seat empty during demonstrations. After just five years on the Phantom, the team then moved on to the Douglas A-4F Skyhawk in 1974. Having completed their 40th season, on November 8, 1986, the team unveiled what would prove to be by far their longest-serving mount: the McDonnell Douglas F/A-18 Hornet.

This would serve until November 8, 2020, when it was finally replaced by the Boeing F/A-18E/F Super Hornet – the team's current aircraft.

One distinctive feature of the team over the years has been its accompanying support aircraft. From 1970 to May 2019, this was a C-130 Hercules known as 'Fat Albert' which made spectacular use of JATO rockets. Since then, 'Fat Albert' has been a C-130J Super Hercules acquired from the RAF.

MODERN AEROBATIC TEAMS **071**

MODERN AEROBATIC TEAMS — CHAPTER 2 – NORTH AMERICA

▼ NORTH AMERICAN F-86F SABRE
North American F-86F Sabre, 51-2884, Minute Men Aerobatic Team, 120th Fighter-Interceptor Squadron, 140th Fighter-Interceptor Group, Colorado Air National Guard, Buckley Field, Colorado, 1958.
The Minute Men operated the Sabre from 1958 until the disbandment of the team in 1959.

▼ NORTH AMERICAN F-86D SABRE DOG
North American F-86D Sabre Dog, 51-6181, Sabre Knights, 325th Fighter-Interceptor Squadron, United States Air Force, Hamilton Air Force Base, California, USA, 1955.
The four-ship team lasted until the squadron's transition to the F-102 Delta Dagger in 1957.

MARINE PHANTOMS AEROBATIC TEAM, USMC

Having received McDonnell FH-1 Phantom twin-jet fighters, the US Marine Corps' VMF-122 Squadron at Cherry Point established a new aerobatic team in early 1949.

Flown initially in standard unit colours, the Phantoms received a new overall sea blue paint job with yellow trim for a performance at the Cleveland National Air Races in September 1949.

A display for the Aviation Writers Association airshow on May 15, 1950, would prove to be one of their last as the team were forced to disband after being hit by the double whammy of transitioning to the McDonnell F2H-1 Banshee and the beginning of the Korean War.

MINUTE MEN, AIR NATIONAL GUARD

Three pilots of the Colorado Air National Guard's 120th Fighter Squadron, flying P-51 Mustangs, began performing together at local fairs and rodeos as an unofficial display team in 1947.

They began to receive more requests for displays and by 1950 event organisers from other states besides Colorado were asking them to attend. This was interrupted when the 120th were sent to fly combat missions during the Korean War but when they returned home, flying new F-80C Shooting Stars, the team re-formed.

Their leader, WW2 veteran Lieutenant Colonel Walter 'Walt' Williams, began looking for a name and 'Minute Men' was suggested – harking back to the National Guard's citizen-soldier roots. The F-80Cs were then each given a new silver and red paint scheme with the team's name painted on the side of their fuselages plus white smoke generators.

By 1956, the team were performing with five F-80Cs and in October 1957 the Minute Men finally became the official Jet Precision Demonstration Team for the Air National Guard. Now they were given a C-47 cargo aircraft to accompany them to performances as well as a permanent crew of mechanics.

The team got seven F-86Fs in 1958 and these were painted in the same colours as the F-80s. They continued to fly displays and went on a ten-day, 5,000-mile tour of Central America in early 1959. Then, on July 10, 1959, the Minute Men gave their final performance at Grand Junction, Colorado, before being disbanded as a cost-saving measure.

MODERN AEROBATIC TEAMS

MODERN AEROBATIC TEAMS CHAPTER 2 – NORTH AMERICA

▼ NORTH AMERICAN F-86F SABRE

North American F-86F Sabre, 53-1201/ FU-201, Skyblazers, 22nd Fighter Squadron, United States Air Force in Europe, Chaumont Airbase, France, 1955.
The Skyblazers were formed from the European-Based 22nd Fighter squadron, using successively the F-80, F-84, F-86 and F-100 aircraft, from 1949 until 1962.

▼ REPUBLIC F-84G THUNDERJET

Republic F-84G Thunderjet, 51-16720, Thunderbirds, 3600th Air Demonstration Team, United States Air Force, Luke Air Force Base, Arizona, 1954.
The Thunderbirds were set up as the 3600th Air Demonstration Team, flying the Thunderjet from 1953 until 1955.

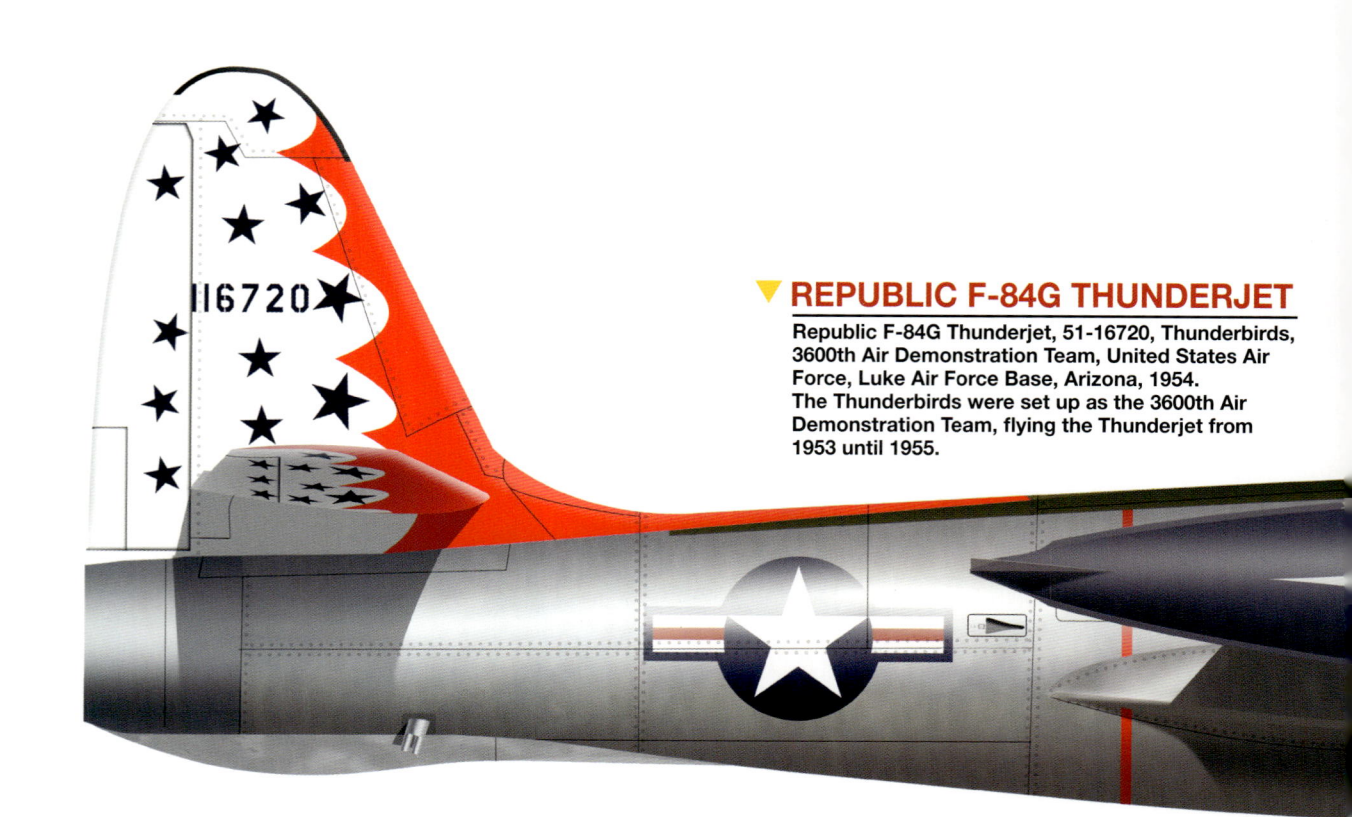

SABRE KNIGHTS, USAF
Pilots of the United States Air Defense Command's 325th Fighter Interceptor Squadron, stationed at Hamilton airbase, decided to set up their own aerobatic display team in April 1954.
The Sabre Knights started out flying F-86F Sabres but had converted to F-86D Sabre Dogs by the end of the year. The team practised hard in their own time but never received official recognition as a USAF display team. The squadron was stood down in August 1955 and this simultaneously put an end to the Sabre Knights.

MODERN AEROBATIC TEAMS   075

MODERN AEROBATIC TEAMS CHAPTER 2 – NORTH AMERICA

▼ REPUBLIC F-105 THUNDERCHIEF
Republic F-105 Thunderchief, 57-5787, Thunderbirds Air Demonstration Squadron, United States Air Force, Nellis Air Force Base, Nevada, 1964.
The Thunderchief was only used for six shows by the team until an accident resulting from structural failure resulted in its replacement.

▼ NORTH AMERICAN F-100C SUPER SABRE
North American F-100C Super Sabre, 55-2723, Thunderbirds Air Demonstration Squadron, United States Air Force, Nellis Air Force Base, Nevada, 1962.
The F-100C was the first supersonic aircraft flown by the team and it would serve for 13 years; it was briefly replaced by the F-105 in 1964, but after an accident with this aircraft, the team replaced it with a new variant of the Super Sabre, the F-100D.

076 MODERN AEROBATIC TEAMS

SKYBLAZERS, USAF

Three pilots from the 22nd Fighter Squadron of the 36th Fighter Wing, based at Fürstenfeldbruk, Germany, began to practice formation flying with their new Lockheed F-80B Shooting Star jets in 1949. A fourth aircraft was then added and the new team flew its first demonstration that October.

Just three months later, in January 1950, the 36th Fighter Wing became the 36th Fighter-Bomber Wing and was reequipped with Republic F-84E Thunderjets. The aerobatic team, now known as the Skyblazers, continued to fly using these new aircraft – their displays lasting around 13 minutes.

They had flown a remarkable 260 demonstrations across 12 countries and been seen by more than 10 million people by the summer of 1952. The team transitioned to flying specially-painted F-86F Sabres in 1954 and two years later switched again, this time to the F-100C Super Sabre. White, blue and red smoke generators were added for the Skyblazers' 1960 season.

They developed a unique manoeuvre that same year: a gear-down diamond pass at low speed, followed by a sudden climb at 45-degrees with full afterburner. Fuel was simultaneously injected into their exhausts, resulting in 8-10m long jets of flame trailing behind each aircraft. Skyblazers indeed! Then, as the diamond was climbing away, a solo F-100 would appear and fly directly through the smoke and flames – trailing its own jet of flames. All of this came to an end when the Skyblazers were disbanded in 1962.

MODERN AEROBATIC TEAMS CHAPTER 2 – NORTH AMERICA

▼ MCDONNELL F-4E PHANTOM
McDonnell F-4E Phantom, 66-0291/4, Thunderbirds, USAF Air Demonstration Squadron, Nellis Air Force Base, Nevada, 1971. The tail of the No. 4 aircraft appeared frequently as if it had been painted black, but this was due to exhaust fumes of the other aircraft when flying in formation.

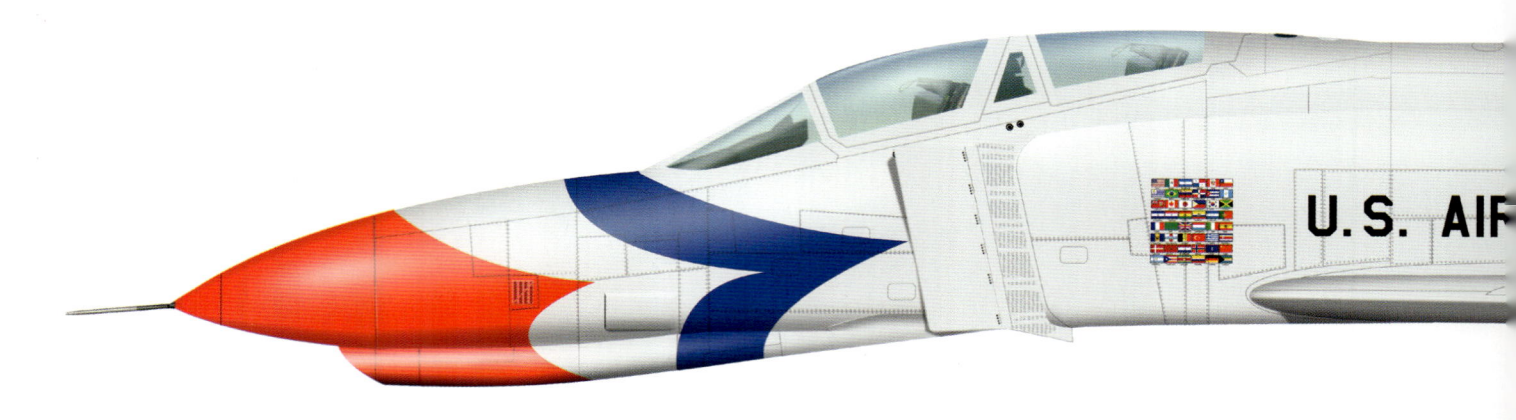

▼ NORTHROP T-38 TALON
Northrop T-38 Talon, 5, Thunderbirds Air Demonstration Squadron, United States Air Force, Nellis Air Force Base, Nevada, 1974. The frugal T-38 became the Thunderbirds' new aircraft in 1974, reportedly as a cost-saving measure. It would be replaced by the F-16 in 1983.

THUNDERBIRDS, USAF

The 3600th Air Demonstration Team was officially activated on May 25, 1953, at Luke airbase, just west of Phoenix, Arizona – having spent six months unofficially training beforehand. They were initially equipped with Republic F-84G Thunderjets, plus a two-seater T-33 Shooting Star for the narrator. They gave 26 performances during their first three months alone.

After less than two years, the team transitioned to swept-wing F-84F Thundersteaks – changing again to the North American F-100C Super Sabre after less than a year. This switch was accompanied by a move to Nellis airbase in Nevada, which made it easier to maintain the aircraft.

A change to the Republic F-105B Thunderchief in 1964 was cut short after structural defects were uncovered in the aircraft. After just six shows, the No. 2 aircraft suffered a catastrophic structural failure during a pitch-up manoeuvre which led to the death of the pilot.

The Thunderbirds subsequently returned to flying Super Sabres, specifically the F-100D, which was retained until 1968. They then converted to the new F-4E Phantom II.

During the oil crisis in 1973 they switched to the T-38 Talon – since it used only a fifth as much fuel as the Phantom. Catastrophe struck on January 18, 1982, when four aircraft collided during a four-plane diamond loop, killing all four pilots. The cause of the accident was traced to a mechanical problem with the No. 1 aircraft's control stick actuator, resulting in the formation leader being unable to exert sufficient pressure on the control stick during the loop. The wing and slot pilots had been taking their visual cue from the leader, rather than paying attention to where they were in relation to the ground.

Aerobatics were suspended for six months during the investigation and at its conclusion the Thunderbirds were reconstituted flying the new General Dynamics F-16A Fighting Falcon in 1983. In 1990, they performed their landmark 3,000th airshow and two years later the team converted to the F-16C/D Block 32. In 2009, the Thunderbirds upgraded again to their current mounts: the F-16C/D Block 52.

Unusually, the team's entire 2013 season was cancelled due to budget cuts resulting from the United States fiscal cliff, before performances recommenced in 2014.

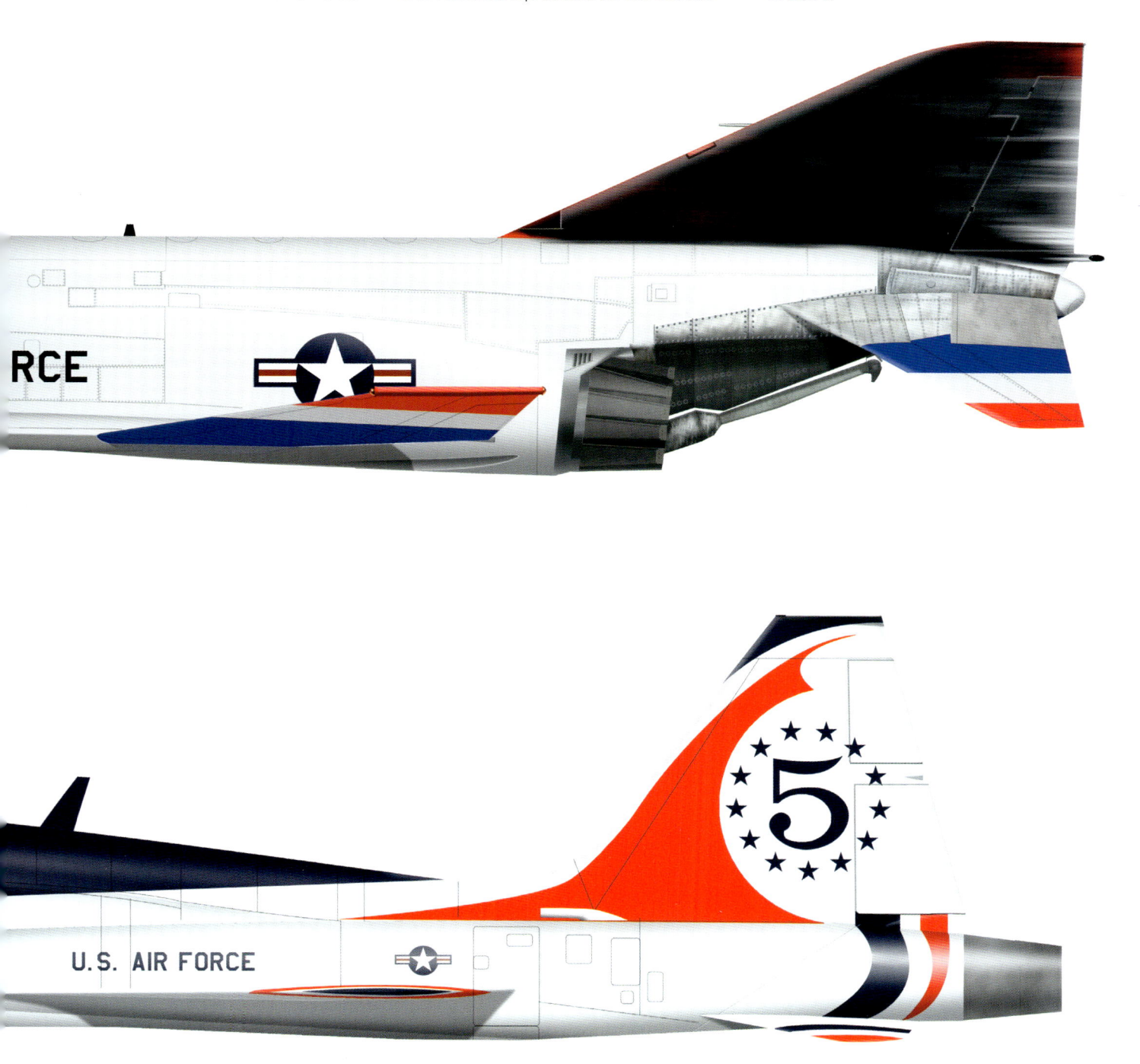

MODERN AEROBATIC TEAMS **079**

MODERN AEROBATIC TEAMS
CHAPTER 2 – NORTH AMERICA

▼ GENERAL DYNAMICS F-16A BLOCK 15
General Dynamics F-16A Block 15, 81-0663/ 1, Thunderbirds Air Demonstration Squadron, Nellis Air Force Base, Nevada, 1984. The Thunderbirds switched to the F-16 in 1983, firstly with the A variant and, beginning in 1992, the C variant.

▼ LOCKHEED C-130A HERCULES
Lockheed C-130A Hercules, 56-0473, Four Horsemen, 774th Troop Carrier Squadron, United States Air Force, Sewart Air Force Base, Tennessee, USA, 1959.
Certainly one of the more unique aerobatic teams, the Four Horsemen flew the mighty Hercules from 1957 until 1960.

FOUR HORSEMEN, USAF
Perhaps the USAF's most unusual aerobatic team flew a quartet of four-engine Lockheed C-130A Hercules transport aircraft. After a cancelled airdrop mission at Fort Campbell, Kentucky, in early 1957, four C-130A crews decided to give formation flying a go. They initially called themselves the Thunder Weasels – a riff on the already famous Thunderbirds and their own squadron patch which featured a picture of a weasel.

However, this name was soon swapped for something more dramatic: the Four Horsemen, as in the biblical four horsemen of the apocalypse.

Their first public show was for the 314th Troop Carrier Wing at Stewart airbase in Tennessee while delivering new C-130s to the base. After that, the four crews were given official status as a demonstration team though they did not have C-130s assigned to them on a permanent basis. A key part of the team's routine was a diamond formation take-off, demonstrating the aircraft's short take-off capability, followed by a diamond formation landing. This all came to an end in 1960 when the team's pilots were all posted away to different airbases.

MODERN AEROBATIC TEAMS **081**

MODERN AEROBATIC TEAMS   CHAPTER 3 – SOUTH/CENTRAL AMERICA

CHAPTER 3 – SOUTH/CENTRAL AMERICA

ARGENTINA

▼ FMA PAMPA II

FMA Pampa II, 1, Cruz del Sur, IV Brigada Aérea, Fuerza Aérea Argentina (Southern Cross, 4th Air Brigade, Argentinian Air Force), El Plumerillo airbase, Mendonza, Argentina, 2013. In 2013 there was a brief attempt to reactivate the Cruz del Sur team, and a solo aircraft was painted in this colour scheme.

CRUZ DEL SUR, ARGENTINIAN AIR FORCE

Celebrations to mark the 50th anniversary of the Argentine Air Force in August 1962 included the establishment of the Cruz del Sur – Southern Cross – aerobatic team in 1961. Formed from the 1st Fighter-Bomber Group of the IV Brigada Aérea at Tamarindo, Mendoza, the team flew six F-86F Sabres in bright blue, red, white and yellow livery. Their first performance was in January 1962 and a further five aircraft were later added for a complement of 11 in total.

The team were disbanded in December 1962 but nevertheless occasional displays were still performed in subsequent years without using the Cruz del Sur name up to 1985, after which the F-86s were retired.

The name was revived, however, in 1997 and applied to a new team flying seven two-seater piston-engine Sukhoi Su-29 AR aerobatic aircraft. This team performed for the first time on March 15, 1998, to celebrate the 49th anniversary of the IV Brigada Aérea but with only two aircraft. Four flew during a parade for Argentina Air Force Day on July 7, 1998, and the team continued to perform in 1999 before apparently being disbanded. A third version of the Cruz del Sur was established in 2013 flying six locally-made IA-63 Pampa II aircraft but this proved to be a short-lived venture and the team has evidently been on hiatus ever since.

▼ NORTH AMERICAN F-86F SABRE

North American F-86F Sabre, C-119, Cruz del Sur, IV Brigada Aérea, Fuerza Aérea Argentina (Southern Cross, 4th Air Brigade, Argentinian Air Force), El Plumerillo airbase, Mendonza, Argentina, 1962.
In 1962, to celebrate the 50th anniversary of the FAA, an aerobatic team was created using Sabres from the IV Brigada Aérea.

MODERN AEROBATIC TEAMS **083**

MODERN AEROBATIC TEAMS
CHAPTER 3 – SOUTH/CENTRAL AMERICA

▼ NORTH AMERICAN T-6 TEXAN

North American T-6 Texan/T-60, 1559/B, Esquadrilha da Fumaça, Academia da Força Aérea, Força Aérea Brasileira (Smoke Squadron, Air Force Academy, Brazilian Air Force), Pirassununga, São Paulo, Brazil, 1964.
The BAF demonstration team was created within the Air Force Academy in 1962; it got its name from the thick smoke generated by the aircraft during exhibitions.

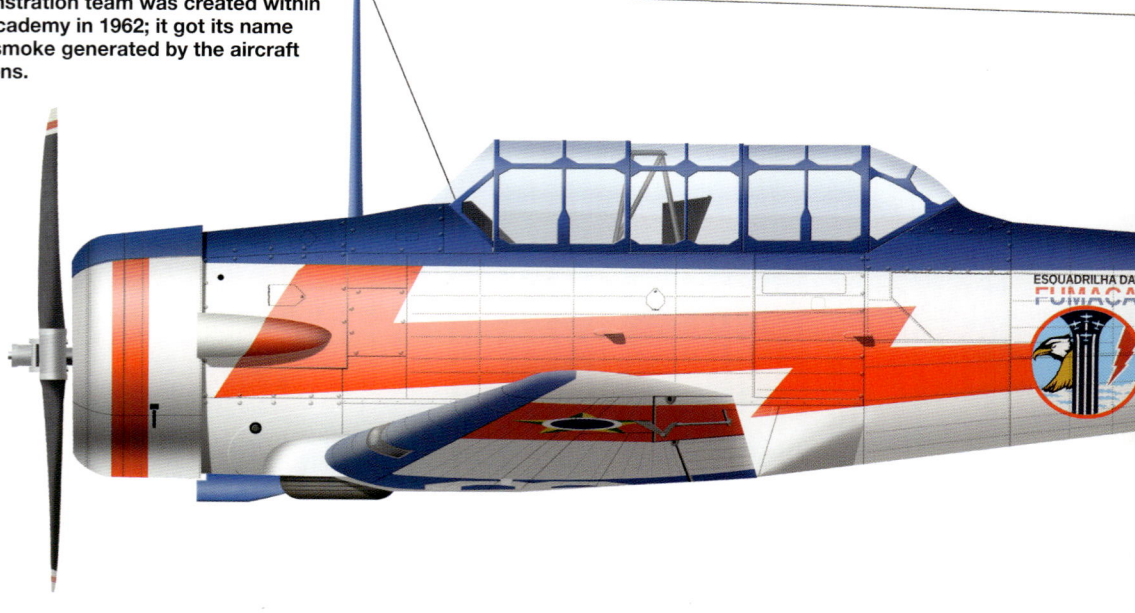

▼ EMBRAER T-27 TUCANO

Embraer T-27 Tucano, 1331, Esquadrilha da Fumaça, Esquadrão de Demonstração Aérea, Academia da Força Aérea, Força Aérea Brasileira (Smoke Flight, Air Demonstration Squadron, Air Force Academy, Brazilian Air Force), Pirassununga, São Paulo, Brazil, 1987.
When the team was re-formed in 1982, it got a new official designation (Esquadrão de Demonstração Aérea – Air display squadron) and a new aircraft: the locally designed and built Embraer T-27 Tucano.

084 MODERN AEROBATIC TEAMS

BRAZIL

ESQUADRILHA DA FUMAÇA, BRAZILIAN AIR FORCE

Brazil's national aerobatic team, officially known simply as the Esquadrão de Demonstração Aérea or Aerial Demonstration Squadron, is unofficially known as Esquadrilha da Fumaça or Smoke Squadron.

Equipped with seven Embraer EMB-314 Super Tucano turboprop trainers, it is stationed at the Brazilian Air Force Academy in Pirassununga, São Paulo. Remarkably, the team's history stretches back to 1952 with their first performance, flying piston-engine North American T-6 Texans, being on May 14 of that year over Copacabana beach. Sixteen years later, in 1968, the team converted to the CM 170-2 Magister, known in Força Aérea Brasileira service as the T-24. Unfortunately, the Magister did not cope well with the hot and humid weather of Brazil and after 46 shows the team reverted back to the T-6, which they continued to use until they were disbanded in 1977 after a grand total of 1,225 shows flying that type.

The team were then re-formed on December 8, 1983, flying Brazilian-made Neiva T-25 Universal piston-engine basic trainers. These were replaced, after 55 displays, with new Embraeer EMB-312 Tucano turboprop-powered trainers painted bright red – and later gloss blue. By 2010, Smoke Squadron had flown more than 2,000 displays using the EMB-312s. Deliveries of new EMB-314 Super Tucanos, the team's current aircraft, commenced on September 30, 2012.

▼ FOUGA CM 170 MAGISTER

Fouga CM 170 Magister/T-24, 1723/559, Esquadrilha da Fumaça, Academia da Força Aérea, Força Aérea Brasileira (Smoke Flight, Air Force Academy, Brazilian Air Force), Pirassununga, São Paulo, Brazil, 1970. Magisters were used by the team from 1968 until 1975. They were replaced by the T-6 for two more years until disbandment in 1977.

▼ EMBRAER A-29B SUPER TUCANO

Embraer A-29B Super Tucano, 5966/7, Esquadrilha da Fumaça, Esquadrão de Demonstração Aérea, Academia da Força Aérea, Força Aérea Brasileira (Smoke Flight, Air demonstration Squadron, Air Force Academy, Brazilian Air Force), Pirassununga, São Paulo, Brazil, 2023.

From 2012 on, the team was equipped with a new aircraft, the Embraer A-29 Super Tucano.

MODERN AEROBATIC TEAMS **085**

MODERN AEROBATIC TEAMS   CHAPTER 3 – SOUTH/CENTRAL AMERICA

CHILE

▼ LOCKHEED F-80C SHOOTING STAR
Lockheed F-80C Shooting Star, J-335, Condores de Plata, Grupo n.º 7, Fuerza Aérea de Chile, (Silver Condors, Group No. 7, Chilean Air Force), Cerrillos airbase, Chile, 1966. The Condores used standard F-80s, in natural metal finish; they performed from 1958 until 1967.

▼ GAMECOMPOSITES GAMEBIRD GB1
GameComposites GameBird GB1, 5, Escuadrilla de Alta Acrobacia Halcones, Fuerza Aérea de Chile, (Falcons High Aerobatic Team, Chilean Air Force), El Bosque airbase, Chile, 2023.
The Escuadrilla de Alta Acrbacia Halcones is the current FAC demonstration unit; it was created in 1981 using first the Pitts Special, then the Extra EA300, next the Extra EA300L and finally the GameBird GB1 from 2021 onwards.

086 MODERN AEROBATIC TEAMS

CONDORES DE PLATA, CHILEAN AIR FORCE

The Condores de Plata, the Silver Condors, were the first aerobatic team of the Chilean Air Force. Formed in 1958 from No. 7 Squadron, the team flew four Lockheed-built F-80 Shooting Stars prior to being disbanded in 1966.

ESCUADRILLA DE ALTA ACROBACIA HALCONES, CHILEAN AIR FORCE

Flying tiny piston-engine tandem two-seater Game Composites GB1 GameBirds, the Escuadrilla de Alta Acrobacia Halcones of the Chilean Air Force – the Hawks – are said to somewhat resemble the RAF's Red Arrows when it comes to flying complex high-risk manoeuvres.

The team was formed on January 14, 1981, flying four Pitts Special aerobatic biplanes with a fifth being added later. These aircraft were flown for around 400 shows both in Chile and abroad before the team switched to the German-made Extra EA300 in 1990.

Again, around 400 performances were made with the EA300s before the team upgraded to the Extra EA300L in 2003.

With these, they performed in airshows all over the world, including displays in Argentina, Belgium, Bolivia, Brazil, Canada, Ecuador, France, Israel, Peru, the United Kingdom and Uruguay. Starting in July 2019, the team received seven GB1 GameBirds – displaying them in public for the first time in 2020.

MODERN AEROBATIC TEAMS **087**

MODERN AEROBATIC TEAMS CHAPTER 3 – SOUTH/CENTRAL AMERICA

EL SALVADOR

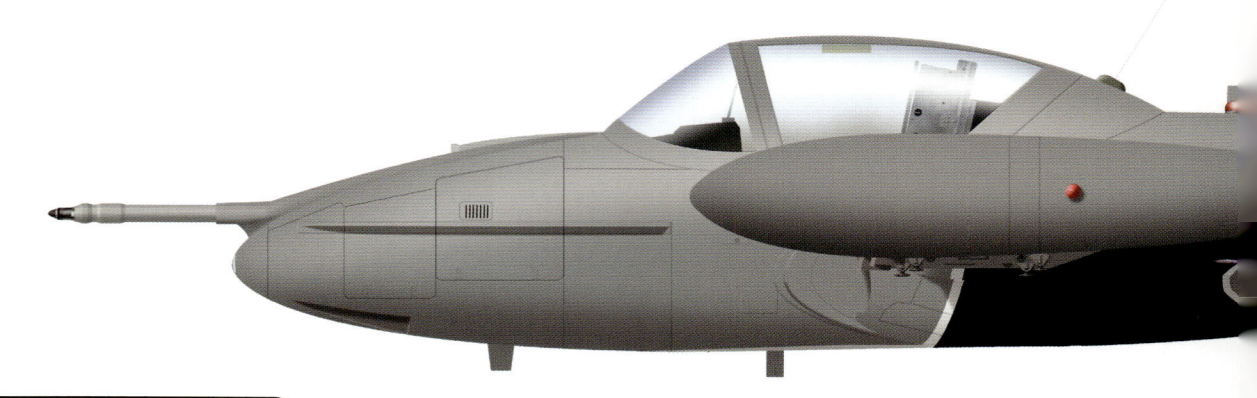

MEXICO

▼ BEECHCRAFT T-6C+ TEXAN II
Beechcraft T-6C+ Texan II, 6603, Equipo Acrobático, Escuela Militar de Aplicación Aero-Táctica de la Fuerza Aérea, Fuerza Aérea Mexicana (Aerobatic Team, Air Force Air-Tactic Application Military School, Mexican Air Force), No 11 Santa Gertrudis Teniente Coronel Juan Pablo Aldasoro Suárez airbase, Saucillo, Mexico, 2016.
The team was funded in 2013 using the aircraft and personnel of its parent unit.

▼ CESSNA A-37B DRAGONFLY

Cessna A-37B Dragonfly, 425, Escuadrilla Cuscatlán, Fuerza Aérea Salvadoreña (Cuscatlán Flight, El Salvador Air Force), Comalapa airbase, El Salvador, 1989.
The original team was wound up in 1980 but returned in 1989 with the A-37 – which they were still flying in 2024.

CUSCATLÁN FLIGHT, EL SALVADOR AIR FORCE

The El Salvador Escuadrilla acrobática was formed in 1959 with five Vought FG-1D Corsair piston-engine fighters. During the late 1970s, the unit was re-equipped with F-51D Mustangs and given the name 'Escuadrilla Cobra'. Another change of aircraft followed at the end of 1978, with Magisters replacing the Mustangs. Two years later, the team were disbanded – only to be reestablished in 1989 as the Escuadrilla Cuscatlán with five A-37B Dragonflies; a formation of four plus a solo. They continue to perform at the time of writing.

▼ PILATUS PC-7

Pilatus PC-7, Equipo Acrobático, Escuadrón Avanzado, Escuela Militar de Aviación, Fuerza Aérea Mexicana (Aerobatic Team, Advanced Squadron, Military Aviation School, Mexican Air Force), No. 5 airbase, Zapopan, Mexico, 2023.
Integrated within the Military Aviation School, this demonstration team uses standard aircraft for its exhibitions.

EQUIPO ACROBÁTICO DEL COLEGIO DEL AIRE, MEXICAN AIR FO RCE

Six instructors from the Mexican Air Force's training academy make up the pilots of the Equipo Acrobático del Colegio del Aire team. Established in 2010, they fly six Pilatus PC-7s and made their first international appearance at Laughlin airbase, Del Rio, Texas, on March 9, 2024.

EQUIPO ACROBÁTICO EMAATFA, MEXICAN AIR FORCE

Mexico's second military display team, Equipo Acrobático EMAATFA, is even newer – having been formed in 2013. EMAATFA is the air force's weapons training school and again the team's pilots are all instructors. The team, which has eight pilots, fly six turboprop-powered Beechcraft T-6C+ Texan II aircraft.
They initially flew five, then expanded to six, but subsequently dropped back down to just four after an accident in 2015. More recently, they have begun to fly six-ship formations once again.

MODERN AEROBATIC TEAMS

MODERN AEROBATIC TEAMS CHAPTER 3 – SOUTH/CENTRAL AMERICA

PERU

▼ AERMACCHI MB-339AP
Aermacchi MB-339AP, 5, Diablos Rojos, Fuerza Aérea del Perú (Red Devils, Peruvian Air Force), Capitán FAP Renán Elías Olivera airbase, Pisco, Peru, 1985.
This team had half a dozen aircraft and performed for a few years in the mid-1980s. In the place usually reserved for the air force roundel is the team's emblem.

VENEZUELA

▼ HUNTING PERCIVAL JET PROVOST T.MK.52
Hunting Percival Jet Provost T.52, E047, Las Águilas, Grupo de Entrenamiento Aéreo, Escuela de Aviación Militar, Fuerza Aérea Venezolana (The Eagles, Air Training Group, Military Aviation School, Venezuelan Air Force), airbase, Venezuela, 1964.
In 1964, two aerobatic teams were created within the Venezuelan Air Force's Academy, one with Jet Provost and the other with Beechcraft T-34 Mentor.

DIABLOS ROJOS, PERUVIAN AIR FORCE

The Diablos Rojos, the Red Devils, aerobatic team of the Peruvian Air Force flew formations of six two-seater Aermacchi MB-339AP jet trainers painted in red and white with blue accents during the mid-1980s. Evidently the team soon fell prey to budget cuts which restricted pilots' flying hours, though Peru retains at least five MB-339s in its inventory today.

LAS ÁGUILAS, VENEZUELAN AIR FORCE

Fifteen Hunting Percival Jet Provost T.52s were delivered to the Venezuelan Air Force in 1962 – making it the force's first advanced jet trainer. Two years later, an aerobatic team known as Las Águilas, the Eagles, was formed at Venezuela's Air Force Academy using Jet Provosts. A second team was simultaneously formed at the academy flying piston-engine Beechcraft T-34 Mentors. Exactly how long these teams lasted is unclear however.

MODERN AEROBATIC TEAMS

MODERN AEROBATIC TEAMS CHAPTER 4 – AFRICA

CHAPTER 4 – AFRICA

EGYPT

MOROCCO

▼ MUDRY CAP 232
Mudry CAP 232, 1/ CN-ABV, Patrouille de la Marche Verte, École Royale de l'Air, Forces Royales Air, (Green March Patrol, Royal Air School, Royal Moroccan Air Force), Marrakesh-Menara Airport, Morocco, 2009. The team perform group take-offs with the aircraft attached together by cords, which are subsequently broken in mid-air.

▼ KARAKORUM K-8E

Karakorum K-8E, 6332/2, Silver Stars, Air College, Egyptian Air Force, Bilbeis airbase, Egypt, 2015.
The K-8Es used by the team are part of a lot of 80 built in Egypt from Chinese-supplied kits. The Silver Stars switched to the K-8E in 2003, having earlier flown standard camouflaged L-29s and then Alpha Jets.

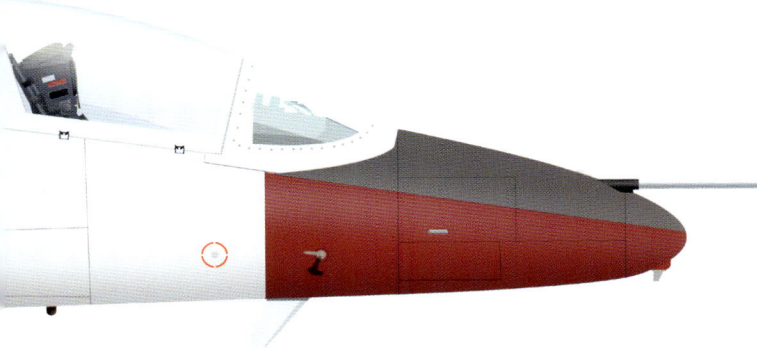

SILVER STARS, EGYPTIAN AIR FORCE

Like many aerobatic teams, Egypt's Silver Stars were formed for a particular occasion – specifically to celebrate the first anniversary of the nation's success in the Yom Kippur War, aka the October War.

The war lasted just under three weeks, from October 6 to October 25, 1973, and the team were established in mid-1974 in readiness for the celebration.

Four instructors from Egypt's Air Force College flew Aero L-29 Delfin jet trainers painted in the air force's standard dark green, brown and yellow camouflage colour scheme. Continuing to perform long after the anniversary event, in 1984 the team was expanded to six aircraft and converted to Alpha Jets. In 1985, the team was expanded still further into a nine-jet formation.

The Silver Stars switched to their current aircraft, the K-8E Karakorum – aka the Chinese Hongdu JL-8 – advanced jet trainer in 2003. Another aircraft was added in 2010 for a total of ten: nine white, red and black painted formation aircraft plus a solo. All are equipped with generators able to produce white, red and blue smoke and rhe team continue to fly displays today.

PATROUILLE DE LA MARCHE VERTE, ROYAL MOROCCAN AIR FORCE

The King of Morocco, Hassan II, commissioned French aerobatic pilot Jean-Pierre Otelli to form an aerobatic display team from the Royal Moroccan Air Force in 1984.

They were named as the Patrouille de la Marche verte, or Green March Patrol, after a peaceful march of 350,000 Moroccan civilian volunteers, led by King Hassan II, to reclaim the disputed Sahara region from Spain in November 1975. Initially flying the piston-engine AS 202 Bravo, made by Swiss firm FFA and Italian company Savoia-Marchetti, they have since flown the CAP 10, CAP 230 and CAP 231. Their most recent aircraft is the CAP 232. The team celebrated their 40th anniversary in 2024.

MODERN AEROBATIC TEAMS **093**

MODERN AEROBATIC TEAMS — CHAPTER 4 – AFRICA

SOUTH AFRICA

BUMBLING BEES, SOUTH AFRICAN AIR FORCE

The commandant of the Flying School at Langebaanweg airbase in South Africa, Chris Prins, decided to form an aerobatic display team in 1953 using four of the school's North American T-6 Harvard trainers.
Exactly why they were subsequently given the name Bumbling Bees is unclear. The team would later transition to the de Havilland Vampire FB.9 – a tropicalised variant of the single-seat F.5 fighter-bomber – and would continue to perform

▼ NORTH AMERICAN T-6 HARVARD

North American T-6 Harvard, 7385/4, Bumbling Bees, Central Flying School, South African Air Force, Langebaanweg airbase, South Africa, 1955.
A display team was formed within the CFS in 1953 using four Harvards trainers; it later transitioned to the de Havilland Vampire and was disbanded in 1967.

▼ PILATUS PC-7 MK.II ASTRA

Pilatus PC-7 MK.II Astra, 3, Silver Falcons, Central Flying School, South African Air Force, Langebaanweg airbase, South Africa, 2009.
The team adopted the title Silver Falcons in 1994 and their new aircraft, the PC-7, in 1999.

until 1967 when the school was moved to Pietersburg airbase. While the school later became the 85th Advanced Training Flying School, Langebaanweg became South Africa's Central Flying School.

SILVER FALCONS, SOUTH AFRICAN AIR FORCE

The origin of the current South African Air Force aerobatic team can be traced back to 1964 when South Africa acquired a licence to build the Aermacchi MB-326 jet trainer. Deliveries of Italian-made pattern aircraft commenced in 1966 and a new firm, Atlas Aircraft Corporation, was then set up to build the South African variant – the MB-326M Impala Mk.I.

With some of the Italian aircraft being delivered to Langebaanweg, commandant Prins decided to use them as the basis of a new display team: the Silver Falcons. Their first show in public was held during the Atlas Aircraft Corporation opening ceremony on November 24, 1967. The four MB-326s were naturally painted silver and had white smoke generators fitted.

Where the Bumbling Bees had been wound up after 14 years, the Silver Falcons persisted and in 1985 their aircraft were repainted in silver, white, orange and blue with their numbers, one to four, painted on in yellow. A fifth aircraft was then added to the team in 1988 as a solo.

The Impalas were repainted again in 1994, this time in silver, blue white and light blue, and a sixth aircraft was added for a performance on May 6, 1994, to mark Nelson Mandela's inauguration as president. The team were relocated to the 85th Combat Flying School at Hoedspruit Airbase in 1995 and at the end of the year they were disbanded.

However, the Silver Falcons were revived in 1999 at Langebaanweg flying four South African licence-made PC-7 Mk.2 Astra trainers. While their new colour scheme left out the silver, being the standard trainer colours of red and white with added numbers on their tails, the aircraft were fitted with white smoke generators.

Nine years later, in 2008, the new Silver Falcons' aircraft finally received a special paint scheme. Three years after that, in December 2012, tragedy struck when the team's cargo aircraft, a C-47TP Dakota in team colours nicknamed Gooney Bird, crashed in the Drakensberg Mountains near Ladysmith, killing the 11 team members on board.

Today the Silver Falcons continue to fly five PC-7 Mk.2s with three additional aircraft maintained as spares.

ACCHI MB-326 IMPALA MK I

MB-326 Impala Mk I, 524/3, Silwer Valke ons), Central Flying School, South African Air nottar airbase, South Africa, 1986.
as established in 1966, using the then newly-ainer jet; this is the colour scheme adopted

MODERN AEROBATIC TEAMS **095**

MODERN AEROBATIC TEAMS — CHAPTER 5 – ASIA

CHAPTER 5 – ASIA

BRUNEI

CHINA

▼ CHENGDU J-7GB

Chengdu J-7GB, 09, August 1st, People's Liberation Army Air Force, People's Liberation Army, Yangcun airbase, People's Republic of China, 2005. The locally designed J-7 (developed from the MiG-21) served the team in two consecutive variants: the J-7EB, in a white and red colour scheme, until 2001 and then the J-7GB, in this white and blue colour scheme, until 2010.

PILATUS PC-7 MARK II
Pilatus PC-7 Mark II, 302/PB, Alap-Alap Formation, Tentera Udara Diraja Brunei (Kestrel Formation, Royal Brunei Air Force), Rimba airbase, Brunei, 2012. The team uses three of the four PC-7s in the RBAF inventory.

ALAP-ALAP FORMATION, ROYAL BRUNEI AIR FORCE
Formed on February 7, 2011, as part of No. 63 Training Squadron stationed at Rimba airbase, the Royal Brunei Air Force's aerobatic team is known as the Alap-Alap Formation, or Kestrel Formation. They fly a trio of PC-7 Mk.2s in white, blue, red and yellow, with each carrying a pair of white smoke pods. They also use the callsign 'Eagle'.

AUGUST 1ST, PEOPLE'S LIBERATION ARMY AIR FORCE
Named after the date of the founding of the People's Liberation Army, August 1st are the aerobatics team of the People's Liberation Army Air Force.
On their founding in 1962 they were equipped with the Shenyang JJ-5, a licence-made version of the Soviet MiG-17 jet fighter. They later transitioned to the Chengdu J-7EB, a licence-made version of the MiG-21 known by the NATO reporting name 'Fishcan'. They traded these in for the upgraded J-7GB in 2001 and then to the Chengdu J-10A fighter in May 2009.
Most recently, in 2023, the team converted to the improved J-10C. Based at Yangcun airbase, near Tianjin, the team generally fly with six aircraft but maintain a fleet of around eight.

MODERN AEROBATIC TEAMS CHAPTER 5 – ASIA

▼ CHENGDU J-10C
Chengdu J-10C, 04, August 1st, People's Liberation Army Air Force, People's Liberation Army, Yangcun airbase, People's Republic of China, 2023. From 2010 onwards, the August 1st team has used the locally-built Chengdu J-10 fighter aircraft in two variants, first the J-10A and now the J-10C.

RED FALCONS, PEOPLE'S LIBERATION ARMY AIR FORCE

A relatively new aerobatic display team, the Red Falcons were formed in 2011 from the Harbin Flying Academy based at Harbin, capital city of Heilongjiang Province.

The team's 18 pilots are all instructors and their eight aircraft are Hongdu JL-8 two-seater jet trainers painted white with blue and red highlights. They are also fitted with generators capable of producing blue, white, yellow and red smoke.

The Red Falcons' debut performance was on September 1, 2011, at an aviation open day in Changchun City in Jilin province.

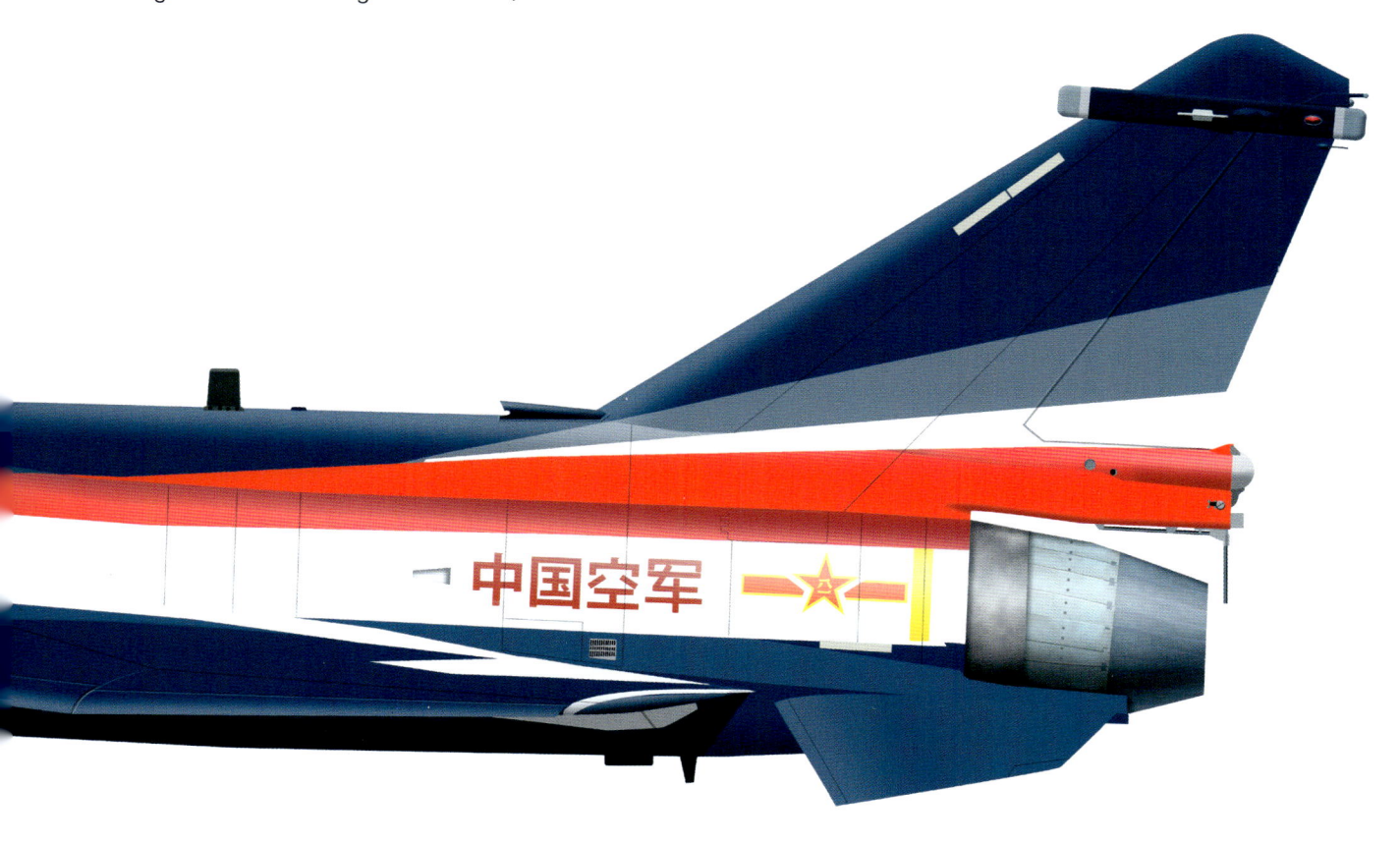

▼ HONGDU JL-8

Hongdu JL-8, 11, Red Falcons, Harbin Flying Academy, People's Liberation Army Air Force, People's Liberation Army, People's Republic of China, 2023. The team was set up in 2011 flying aircraft from the Harbin Flying Academy.

MODERN AEROBATIC TEAMS

MODERN AEROBATIC TEAMS — CHAPTER 5 – ASIA

INDIA

▼ HAWKER HUNTER F.56
Hawker Hunter F.56, A484, Thunderbolts, No. 20 Squadron, Indian Air Force, Pathankot airbase, Punjab, India, 1988.
To celebrate the Golden Jubilee of the IAF in 1982, a team was created from No. 20 Squadron flying Hawker Hunters.

SAGAR PAWAN, INDIAN NAVY

An aerobatic team flying four HJT-16 Kiran Mk.II jet trainers was established by the Indian Navy in 2003 at Dabolim Navai Air Station in Goa, Southern India, in early 2003. They were named Sagar Pawan – Sea Breeze. The first demonstration to feature their dark blue and white-painted aircraft took place in May of that year and included white, red and blue smoke. During an airshow at Bowenpally, near Begumpet airport, on March 3, 2010, one of the team's HJT-16s crashed into buildings, killing the pilot and co-pilot and injuring four people on the ground. The team was subsequently disbanded.

THUNDERBOLTS, INDIAN AIR FORCE

The Golden Jubilee of the Indian Air Force in 1982 saw the formation of a new team flying Hawker Hunter F.56As. Drawn from No. 20 Squadron, the Thunderbolts' nine aircraft were painted in a striking, jagged, dark blue and white 'thunderbolt' scheme. The team was re-equipped with four Indian-built HAL HJT-16 Kiran Mk.II jet trainers in 1990.

▼ HAL HJT-16 KIRAN MK.II

HAL HJT-16 Kiran MK.II, IN078, Sagar Pawan (Sea Breeze), Indian Navy Air Squadron 551, Indian Naval Air Arm, Indian Navy, Dabolim Nava Air Station, Goa, India, 2010.
The team, created in 2001, was initialled called Sagar Kiran (Oceanic Ray of Light).

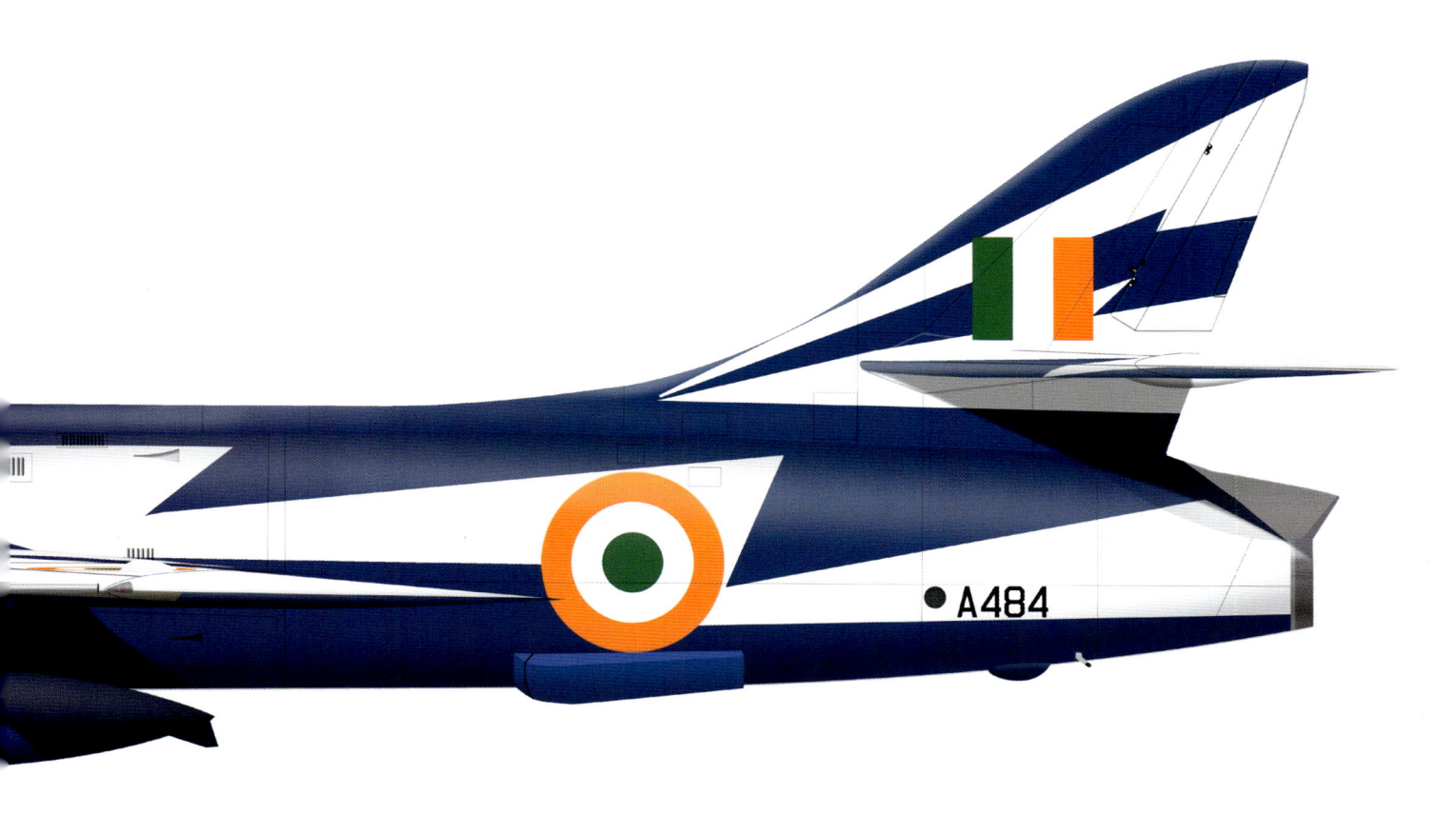

MODERN AEROBATIC TEAMS **101**

MODERN AEROBATIC TEAMS   CHAPTER 5 – ASIA

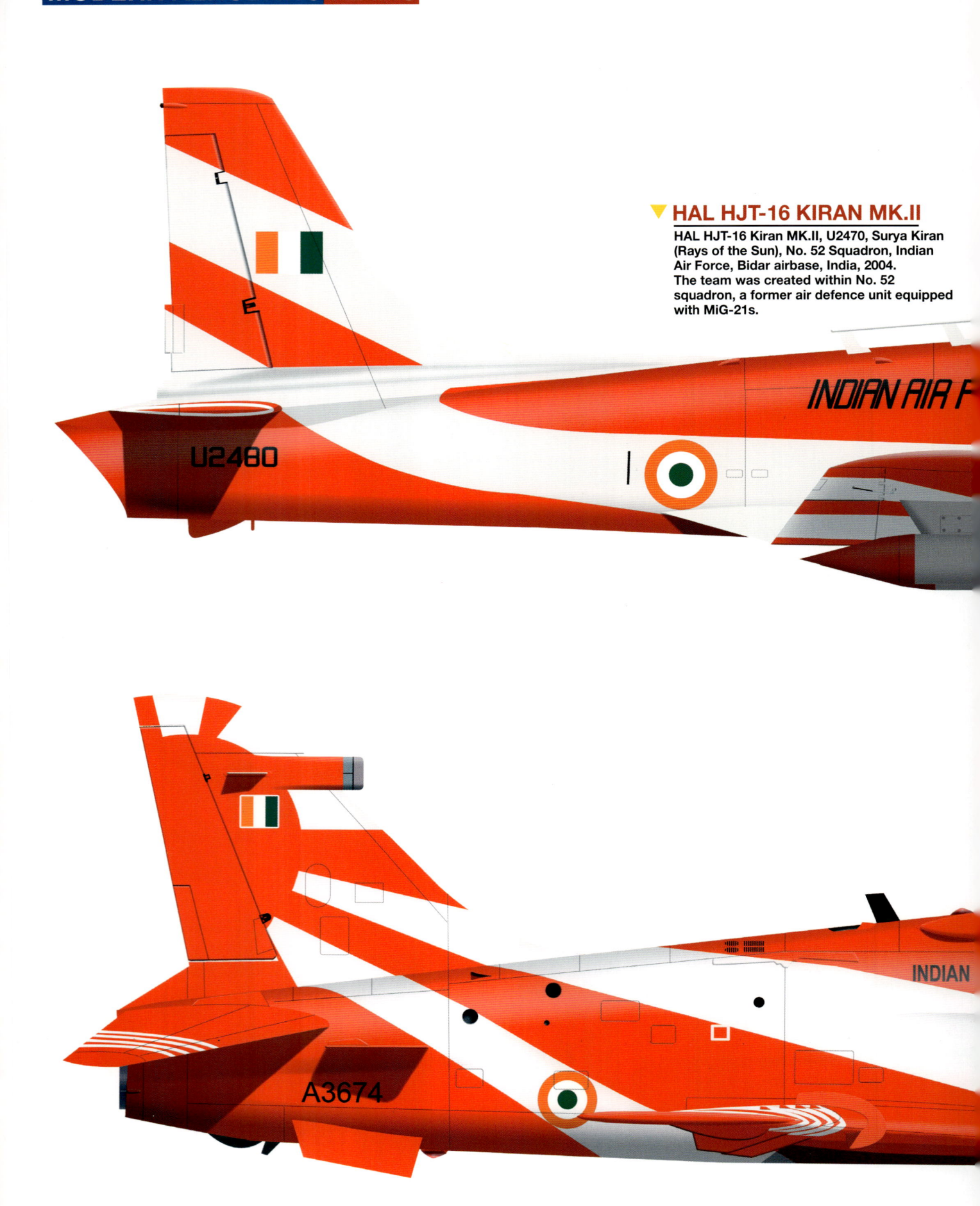

▼ HAL HJT-16 KIRAN MK.II
HAL HJT-16 Kiran MK.II, U2470, Surya Kiran (Rays of the Sun), No. 52 Squadron, Indian Air Force, Bidar airbase, India, 2004. The team was created within No. 52 squadron, a former air defence unit equipped with MiG-21s.

102   MODERN AEROBATIC TEAMS

SURYA KIRAN, INDIAN AIR FORCE

The Thunderbolts were reorganised on May 27, 1996, as a six-ship team plus an additional HJT-16 as a spare. As part of this revision, they got a new name too: Surya Kirin, or 'Rays of the Sun'. Their first performance under this new moniker was for the Indian Air Force Day celebrations on October 8, 1996, and in 1997 the team grew in size to nine aircraft including a solo pair.

The team's foreign debut was in Colombo, Sri Lanka, in 2001. After another nine years of demonstrations, on February 9-13, 2010, they gave a last performance at the Aero India airshow in Bangalore before being disbanded. Their aircraft were reallocated to training units and the 13 pilots themselves were dispersed to other IAF squadrons. However, the Surya Kiran team returned at the beginning of 2015 flying BAe Hawk Mk.132 advanced jet trainers. Their first public display, with four aircraft, was again for India's Air Force Day, on October 8, 2015. By November 2016, the team had been increased to six Hawks and by 2018 this had been increased again to nine. Stationed at Bidar airbase, the team continue to perform today.

▼ BAE HAWK MK.132

Bae Hawk MK.132, A3674, Surya Kiran (Rays of the Sun), No. 52 Squadron, Indian Air Force, Bidar airbase, India, 2022.
The current aircraft of the Surya Kiran is the BAe Hawk, which entered service in 2005.

MODERN AEROBATIC TEAMS

MODERN AEROBATIC TEAMS CHAPTER 5 – ASIA
INDONESIA

▼ BAE HAWK MK.53
BAe Hawk Mk.53, LL-5319, Spirit 85, Skadron Udara 15, Tentara Nasional Indonesia Angkatan Udara (15 Squadron, Indonesian Air Force), Iswahyudi airbase, Java, Indonesia, 1985.
In 1985 a new team was set up by 15 Squadron, using the unit's Hawks.

▼ GENERAL DYNAMICS F-16A FIGHTING FALCON
General Dynamics F-16A Fighting Falcon, TS-1610, Elang Biru, Skadron Udara 3, Tentara Nasional Indonesia Angkatan Udara (Blue Eagle, 3 squadron, Indonesian Air Force), Iswahyudi airbase, Java, Indonesia, 1995.
Created in 1995, the team flew until 2000.

CAC SABRE

CAC Sabre, 03, Spirit 78, TS-8603, Skadron Udara 14, Tentara Nasional Indonesia Angkatan Udara (14 squadron, Indonesian Air Force), Iswahyudi airbase, Java, Indonesia, 1978.
Taking its name from the year it was founded, this team used aircraft from 14 Squadron.

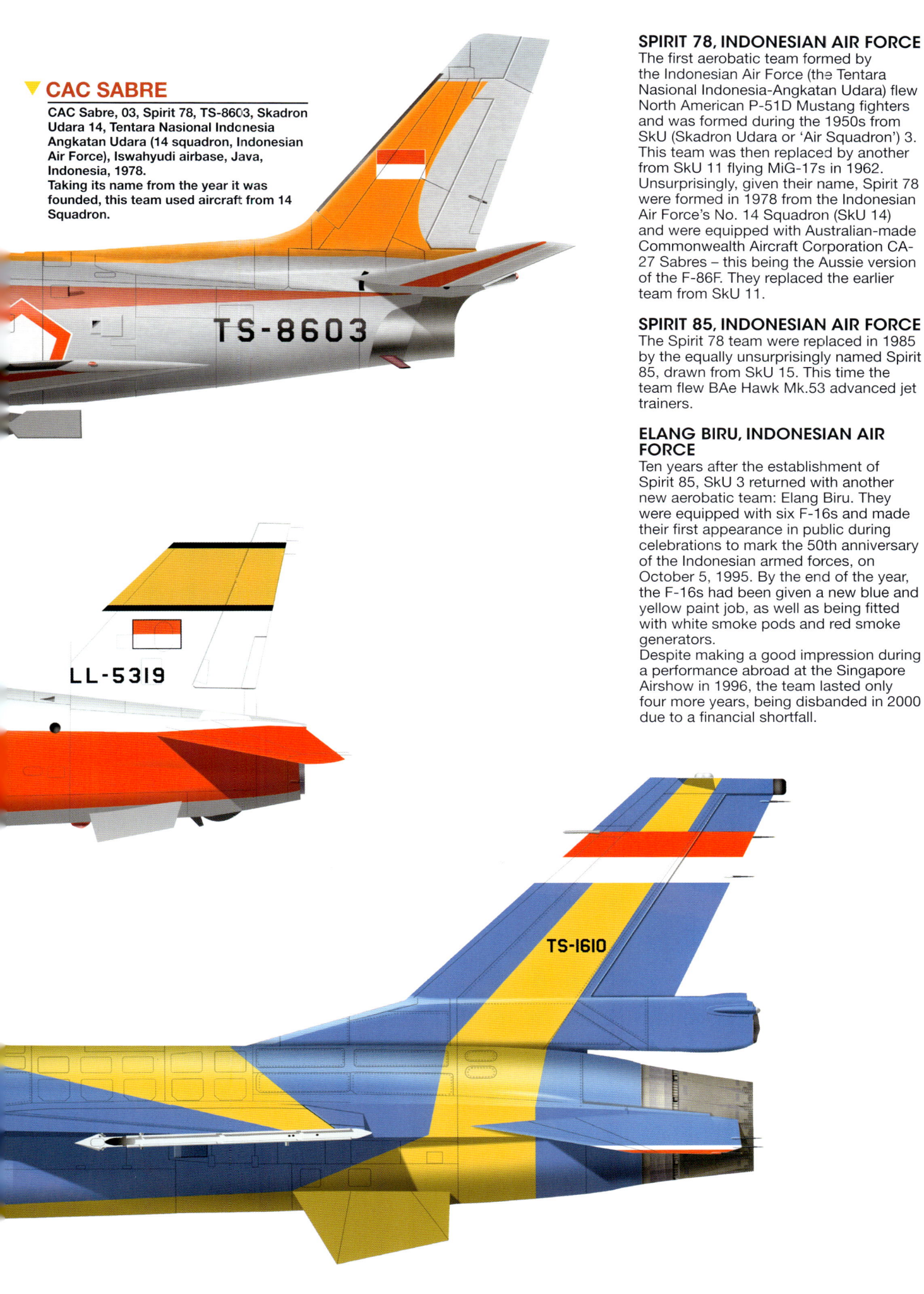

SPIRIT 78, INDONESIAN AIR FORCE
The first aerobatic team formed by the Indonesian Air Force (the Tentara Nasional Indonesia-Angkatan Udara) flew North American P-51D Mustang fighters and was formed during the 1950s from SkU (Skadron Udara or 'Air Squadron') 3. This team was then replaced by another from SkU 11 flying MiG-17s in 1962. Unsurprisingly, given their name, Spirit 78 were formed in 1978 from the Indonesian Air Force's No. 14 Squadron (SkU 14) and were equipped with Australian-made Commonwealth Aircraft Corporation CA-27 Sabres – this being the Aussie version of the F-86F. They replaced the earlier team from SkU 11.

SPIRIT 85, INDONESIAN AIR FORCE
The Spirit 78 team were replaced in 1985 by the equally unsurprisingly named Spirit 85, drawn from SkU 15. This time the team flew BAe Hawk Mk.53 advanced jet trainers.

ELANG BIRU, INDONESIAN AIR FORCE
Ten years after the establishment of Spirit 85, SkU 3 returned with another new aerobatic team: Elang Biru. They were equipped with six F-16s and made their first appearance in public during celebrations to mark the 50th anniversary of the Indonesian armed forces, on October 5, 1995. By the end of the year, the F-16s had been given a new blue and yellow paint job, as well as being fitted with white smoke pods and red smoke generators.
Despite making a good impression during a performance abroad at the Singapore Airshow in 1996, the team lasted only four more years, being disbanded in 2000 due to a financial shortfall.

MODERN AEROBATIC TEAMS

MODERN AEROBATIC TEAMS CHAPTER 5 – ASIA

▼ GENERAL DYNAMICS F-16A FIGHTING FALCON
General Dynamics F-16A Fighting Falcon, TS-1611, Jupiter Blue, Tentara Nasional Indonesia Angkatan Udara (Indonesian Air Force), Iswahyudi airbase, Java, Indonesia, 2001.
A composite formation was created from the Elang Biru (F-16) and Jupiter (BAe Hawk) teams in 2001; the next year, following a mid-air collision, it ceased flying. The aircraft flew in standard camouflage colours.

▼ KAI KT-1B WOONGBI
KAI KT-1B Woongbi, LL0110, Jupiter Team, Skadron Pendidikan 102, Tentara Nasional Indonesia Angkatan Udara (No.102 Training Squadron, Indonesian Air Force), Adisutjipto airbase, Java, Indonesia, 2022.
The current TNI-AU demonstration team fly the KT-1.

JUPITER AEROBATIC TEAM, INDONESIAN AIR FORCE

The current Indonesian Air Force aerobatic display team, Jupiter was formed from Skadik 103 in 1996. Equipped with BAe Hawk Mk.53 jet trainers, they made their first performance on September 23, 1997.

Four years later, Jupiter Team merged with elements of the recently defunct Elang Biru to become Jupiter Blue. Their fleet now included three Hawk Mk.53s, one Hawk Mk.109 and two F-16s – all painted in grey camouflage colours except for the Hawk Mk.109, which had olive-brown camouflage. The Hawks carried red and blue smoke generators, while the F-16s had white smoke generators.

Two of the Hawk Mk.53s were involved in a mid-air collision on March 28, 2002, near Iswahyudi airbase – resulting in the deaths of four pilots and then the dissolution of the team.

Six years later, in 2008, the Jupiter Aerobatic Team (JAT for short) was resurrected flying four Korean Aerospace Industries KT-1B Woongbi turboprop-powered trainers. Their first public show took place at Yogyakarta on July 4, 2008, with another at Jakarta that November.

In 2010, JAT undertook a training programme with the Australian Roulettes team – with two JAT pilots travelling to Australia to observe and fly practice sessions with the Aussies. The six Roulettes then gave a performance at Halim airbase, Jakarta, each with a JAT pilot in the back seat of their PC-9 during their pre-show practice.

JAT was expanded to six aircraft in 2011 and all were given new red and white livery derived from the Indonesian flag. The six-ship performed for the first time on March 16, 2011.

JAT continue to perform today with all pilots being instructors.

MODERN AEROBATIC TEAMS

MODERN AEROBATIC TEAMS CHAPTER 5 – ASIA

IRAN

▼ REPUBLIC F-84G THUNDERJET
Republic F-84G Thunderjet, Golden Crown aerobatic team, Imperial Iranian Air Force, Mehrabad International Airport, Tehran, Iran, 1960. The first aircraft flown by the Golden Crown team was the Thunderjet.

▼ NORTHROP F-5E TIGER II
Northrop F-5E Tiger II, 3-7099/1, Golden Crown aerobatic team, Imperial Iranian Air Force, Mehrabad International Airport, Tehran, Iran, 1978.
The F-5 was the aircraft being used by the team at the point of its dissolution in 1979, first in the F-5A variant and then the F-5E.

MODERN AEROBATIC TEAMS

GOLDEN CROWN, IMPERIAL IRANIAN AIR FORCE

Iran's Golden Crown team was founded after 14 pilots of the Imperial Iranian Air Force were sent to Fürstenfeldbruck Airbase in Germany for jet training in 1958. While nine returned home after two months, the other five remained to receive further training as instructors. One of the five, Nader Jahanbani, saw the USAFE's Skyblazers practising at Fürstenfeldbruck and was inspired to form an Iranian equivalent.

Jahanbani secured permission from the Shah and formed the team flying four F-84Gs. Dozens of training sessions followed before the team's first aerobatic display later that year. In 1959, a further five aircraft were added to allow for nine-ship formations. The team then transitioned to the F-86 in 1961 and continued to fly it until 1968, when they upgraded to the F-5A Freedom Fighter. These would be traded in for F-5E Tiger IIs before the team's dissolution as a result of the Iranian Revolution in 1979. It was reported in February 2020 that a new aerobatic team had been formed, or was being formed, by the Islamic Republic of Iran Air Force – flying three locally-made HESA Kowsar fighters. The Kowsar is based on the F-5 and may indeed utilise old F-5 airframes as part of the manufacturing process.

▼ NORTH AMERICAN F-86 SABRE
North American F-86 Sabre, Golden Crown aerobatic team, Imperial Iranian Air Force, Mehrabad International Airport, Tehran, Iran, 1962.
From 1961 until 1968, the team used the Sabre; in 1963 a fatal collision occurred during a training session.

▼ NORTHROP F-5F/HESA KOWSAR
Northrop F-5F/HESA Kowsar, Islamic Republic of Iran Air Force, Iran, 2020.
It was announced in 2020 that three Kowsars (locally upgraded F-5Fs) would provide the basis for a new Iranian display team. No further details are known.

MODERN AEROBATIC TEAMS **109**

MODERN AEROBATIC TEAMS CHAPTER 5 – ASIA

ISRAEL

▼ FOUGA CM 170 MAGISTER
Fouga CM 170 Magister/IAI Tzukit, 212, Air Force Academy, Israel Defence Forces- Air Force, Hatzerim airbase, Israel, 1970.
Flight demonstration were made at the Air Force Academy in the early 1950s using piston-engined aircraft; the team began using the jet-powered Tzukit in the 1960s.

▼ BEECHCRAFT T-6A EFRONI
Beechcraft T-6A Efroni, 484, IAF Aerobatic Team, Flight Academy, Israeli Air Force, Hatzerim airbase, Israel, 2019.
The team is made up of four aircraft and mainly performs at graduation ceremonies or Air Force Day events.

IAF AEROBATIC TEAM, ISRAELI AIR FORCE

Following accidents resulting from attempts at formation aerobatics during the early 1950s, the IAF decided to formally establish a properly trained display team. Based at the Flight Academy at the Hatzerim airbase, the new team put on its first show flying T-6 Harvards.

They transitioned to the Magister (known as the IAI Tzukit in Israeli service) painted in blue and white at the beginning of the 1960s, before a repaint saw the aircraft appearing in red and white instead. The team would continue to fly Tzukits for an astonishing 50 years – although they were substantially modified and upgraded during that time.

Eventually, in June 2010, the IAF Aerobatic Team switched to the Beechcraft T-6A Texan II (known as the Efroni to the Israelis) turboprop trainer.

MODERN AEROBATIC TEAMS

MODERN AEROBATIC TEAMS CHAPTER 5 – ASIA

JAPAN

▼ NORTH AMERICAN F-86F SABRE

North American F-86F Sabre, 82-7847, Blue Impulse aerobatic team, 1st Air Wing, Japanese Air Self Defense Force, Hamamatsu Airbase, Japan, 1960. The Blue Impulse team flew Sabres from 1960 until 1982; this was their first colour scheme.

BLUE IMPULSE, JAPANESE AIR SELF DEFENSE FORCE

The first Japanese aerobatic team were established, unofficially, at Hamamatsu airbase in 1958. They four F-86F Sabres made under licence by Mitsubishi in standard service colours and were disbanded after just four displays. However, a visit from the USAF's Thunderbirds in 1959 inspired the Japanese to create their own equivalent and a new team was formed at Hamamatsu flying five F-86Fs – three of the pilots having previously been members of the unofficial team a year earlier.

Initially known as Tenryu after a river near their base, the team flew their first demonstration on March 4, 1960, and their name was subsequently changed to Blue Impulse because westerners found it difficult to pronounce Tenryu correctly. Each of the silver, blue and pink F-86Fs was fitted with a generator capable of producing five different colours: white, red, blue, green and yellow. The following year, the aircraft were repainted in overall white with blue highlights.

After a total of 545 displays, the team transitioned to the Mitsubishi T-2 supersonic jet trainer in February 1982. Another 175 demonstrations followed in the T-2 before, in December 1995, it was swapped for the Kawasaki T-4 – the team's current aircraft.

The team made their foreign debut at Nellis airbase in Nevada, USA, in 1997 – every show up to that point having been flown in Japan. The Tohoku earthquake and tsunami caused heavy damage to the team's Matsushima base on March 11, 2011, but the team themselves were unaffected since they had been at Ashiya airbase in Fukuoka at the time for a performance.

Following repairs, Blue Impulse returned home on March 30, 2013.

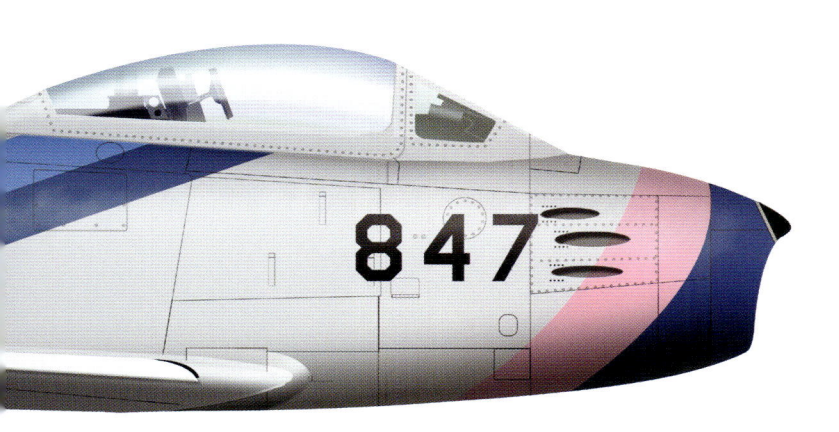

▼ NORTH AMERICAN F-86F SABRE

North American F-86F Sabre, 92-7929, Blue Impulse aerobatic team, 1st Air Wing, Japanese Air Self Defense Force, Hamamatsu Airbase, Japan, 1977. This was the second colour scheme worn by Blue Impulse's Sabres.

▼ KAWASAKI T-4

Kawasaki T-4, 06-5790/5, Blue Impulse aerobatic team, 11 Squadron, 4th Air Wing, Japanese Air Self Defense Force, Matsushima Airbase, Japan, 2006.
The T-4 is the current aircraft flown by the Blue Impulse team.

MODERN AEROBATIC TEAMS **113**

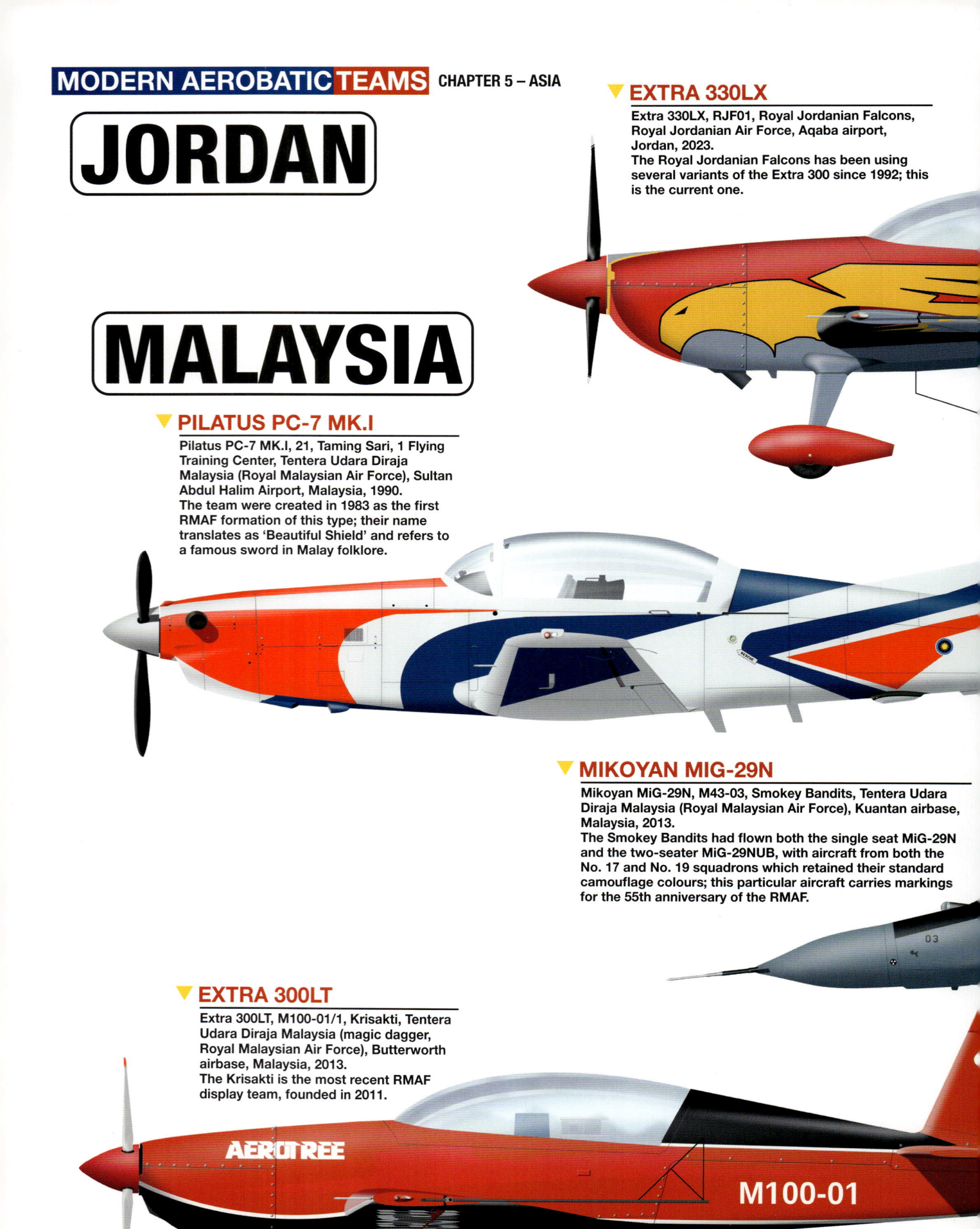

MODERN AEROBATIC TEAMS — CHAPTER 5 – ASIA

JORDAN

MALAYSIA

▼ EXTRA 330LX

Extra 330LX, RJF01, Royal Jordanian Falcons, Royal Jordanian Air Force, Aqaba airport, Jordan, 2023.
The Royal Jordanian Falcons has been using several variants of the Extra 300 since 1992; this is the current one.

▼ PILATUS PC-7 MK.I

Pilatus PC-7 MK.I, 21, Taming Sari, 1 Flying Training Center, Tentera Udara Diraja Malaysia (Royal Malaysian Air Force), Sultan Abdul Halim Airport, Malaysia, 1990.
The team were created in 1983 as the first RMAF formation of this type; their name translates as 'Beautiful Shield' and refers to a famous sword in Malay folklore.

▼ MIKOYAN MIG-29N

Mikoyan MiG-29N, M43-03, Smokey Bandits, Tentera Udara Diraja Malaysia (Royal Malaysian Air Force), Kuantan airbase, Malaysia, 2013.
The Smokey Bandits had flown both the single seat MiG-29N and the two-seater MiG-29NUB, with aircraft from both the No. 17 and No. 19 squadrons which retained their standard camouflage colours; this particular aircraft carries markings for the 55th anniversary of the RMAF.

▼ EXTRA 300LT

Extra 300LT, M100-01/1, Krisakti, Tentera Udara Diraja Malaysia (magic dagger, Royal Malaysian Air Force), Butterworth airbase, Malaysia, 2013.
The Krisakti is the most recent RMAF display team, founded in 2011.

114 MODERN AEROBATIC TEAMS

ROYAL JORDANIAN FALCONS, ROYAL JORDANIAN AIR FORCE

King Hussein of Jordan ordered the formation of a national aerobatic demonstration team led by two experienced pilots, Dave Rahm and Steve Wolf, in 1976.

The pair then began both to perform and to train additional pilots. They initially flew Pitts S-2A Specials but Rahm, a Canadian, was killed when his machine crashed during a performance for the king the following year.

Despite this tragedy, the team continued to train and had racked up 400 flying hours by September 1978. Their first public display took place in October 1978 at the Middle East Civil Aviation Conference in Amman. They then made their first international performance at Doha, Qatar.

The team, by now known as the Royal Jordanian Falcons, acquired a third S-2A Special in 1979, and flew alongside the British Red Arrows at RIAT that year. Since then, the Falcons have been a regular fixture on the international display circuit. They upgraded to Extra EA300s in 1992 then Extra 300Ls in 2007. Today, the team perform with four 330LXs. Originally based at Amman Civil Airport, they have since moved to Aqaba Airport, also known as King Hussein International Airport.

TAMING SARI, ROYAL MALAYSIAN AIR FORCE

The first aerobatic team formed by the Royal Malaysian Air Force was Taming Sari or 'Beautiful Shield'. Its pilots were drawn from the RMAF academy at Alor Setar, Kedah, and they flew five Pilatus PC-7 Mk I trainers painted white, red and blue.

The team's fleet was subsequently reduced to three aircraft and in 1995 two of them suffered a mid-air collision. Both pilots escaped unharmed but the team was then disbanded before the end of the year.

SMOKEY BANDITS, ROYAL MALAYSIAN AIR FORCE

Two years after the dissolution of Taming Sari, in 1997, a new official RMAF aerobatic team was stood up – the Smokey Bandits. In a dramatic turnaround, it was decided that the team should be equipped with five MiG-29 fighters – a mix of single-seat MiG-29Ns and two-seater MiG-29NUBs – in a standard grey camouflage scheme. All of the team's pilots are operational fighter pilots from No. 17 Skn and No. 19 Skn based at Kuantan. However, aerobatic displays ceased in 2013 in order to preserve the number of hours remaining on the MiG-29 airframes, which were then retired in 2017.

KRISAKTI, ROYAL MALAYSIAN AIR FORCE

The most recent official RMAF display team is Krisakti or 'Magic Dagger'.

Formed in 2011 at based at RMAF Butterworth, they flew four Extra 300Ls provided by Malaysian aviation services company Aerotree. Despite initial enthusiasm for their performances, the team do not seem to have been active in recent years.

MODERN AEROBATIC TEAMS **115**

MODERN AEROBATIC TEAMS — CHAPTER 5 – ASIA

PAKISTAN

▼ CESSNA T-37

Cessna T-37, 368, Sherdils (Lion Hearts), Pakistan Air Force Academy, Pakistan Air Force, Risalpur Pakistan, 1977.
The Sherdils were created in 1972; this aircraft is shown with the first colour scheme used.

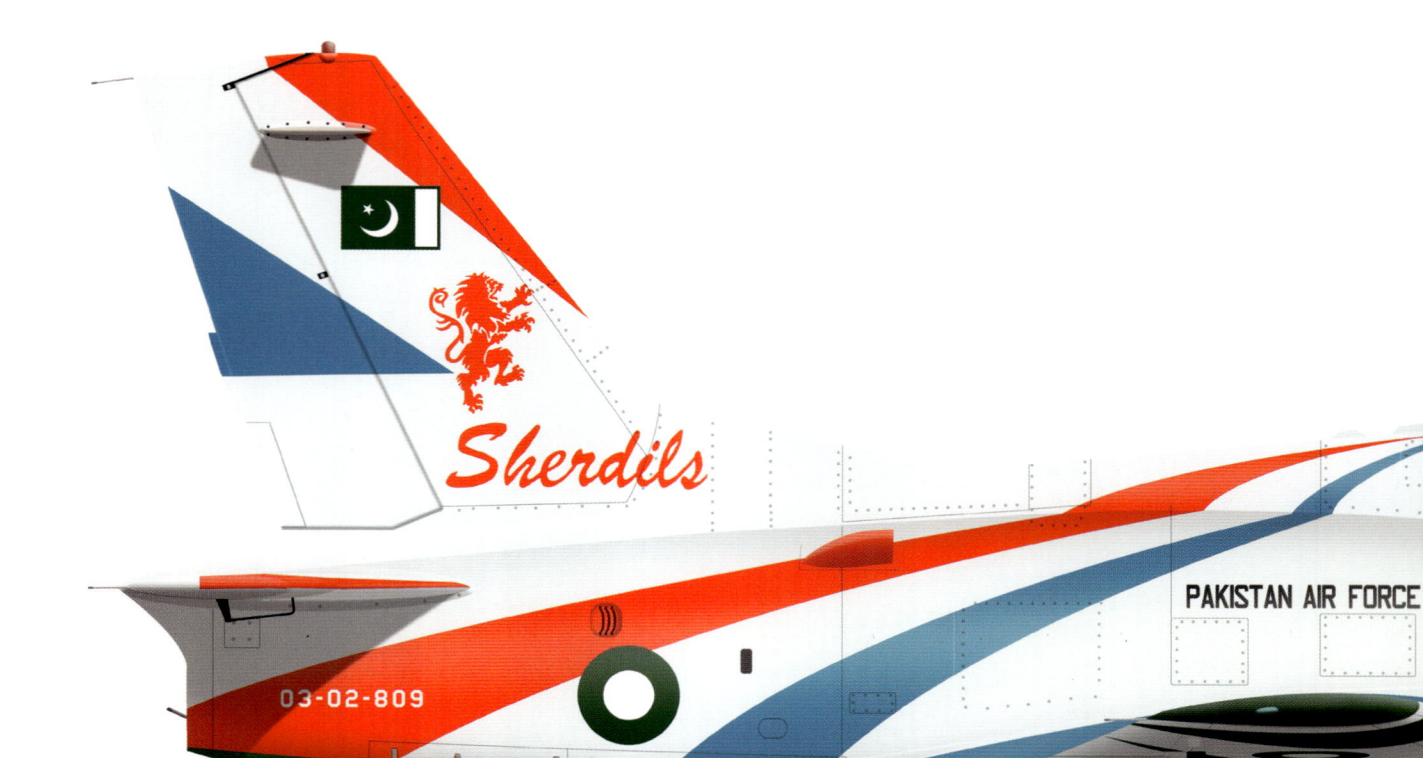

116　MODERN AEROBATIC TEAMS

SHERDILS, PAKISTAN AIR FORCE

Having undertaken an exchange tour at RAF College, Cranwell, Squadron Leader Bahar-ul-haq had seen the Red Pelicans aerobatic team in action and decided that Pakistan should have its own equivalent. The result, in August 1972, was a team known unofficially as the 'Tweety Birds', since they flew four red Cessna T-37 Tweet jet trainers.

The team got their official name, Sherdils or 'Lion Hearts' on September 19, 1974, and would continue to fly their quartet of Tweets for the next 30 years. Not long after their formation, the team's livery was changed to bare metal finish with Day-Glo orange highlights. In 1980, a new white scheme with a red 'sunburst' pattern was adopted. This was then changed to a white, red and blue scheme.

In early 2004 the team were increased to six T-37s, enabling them to expand their repertoire of aerobatic manoeuvres to include loops and barrel rolls in delta formation. On October 2, 2004, the team grew for a second time to nine aircraft. Five years later, the team transitioned to its new aircraft: the Karakoram K-8P aka Hongdu JL-8 jet trainer, starting off with four aircraft. The following year, the formation was brought up seven aircraft, then up to its full strength of nine. Like the T-37s, the K-8Ps were painted in the overall white colour scheme with red and blue stripes.

August 14, 2017, saw the team switch to an experimental new livery: an all-white fuselage with a green stripe on the upper fuselage from nose to tail, plus an all-green fin decorated with a large crescent and star. The same design was also painted on the green underside of the aircraft.

Later, the team reverted back to their white, blue and red, though the new pattern was retained on their undersides.

▼ KARAKORUM K-8P

Karakorum K-8P, 03-02-809, Sherdils (Lion hearts), Pakistan Air Force Academy, Pakistan Air Force, Risalpur, Pakistan, 2023.
K-8P jet trainers have been flown by the Sherdils since 2009; the current team formation has nine aircraft and this is the latest colour scheme used.

MODERN AEROBATIC TEAMS

MODERN AEROBATIC TEAMS
CHAPTER 5 – ASIA

PHILIPPINES

▼ NORTHROP F-5A FREEDOM FIGHTER
Northrop F-5A Freedom Fighter, 10505, Blue Diamonds, 7h Tactical Fighter Squadron, Hukbong Himpapawid ng Pilipinas (Philippines Air Force), Basa Airbase, Philippines, 1970.
The Blue Diamonds used the F-5 in two periods; from 1968 until 1978; and then again, from reactivation in 1986, until their final disbandment in 2005.

▼ NORTH AMERICAN F-86F SABRE
North American F-86F Sabre, 24904, Hot Stuff, Golden Sabres, 9th Tactical Fighter Squadron, Hukbong Himpapawid ng Pilipinas (Philippines Air Force), Basa Airbase, Philippines, 1973.
The Golden Sabres were set up in 1972 but lasted only for a year before being merged with another display team, the Red Aces, to form the Sabres.

118 MODERN AEROBATIC TEAMS

NORTH AMERICAN F-86F SABRE

North American F-86F Sabre, 113432, Blue Diamonds, 7h Tactical Fighter Squadron, Hukbong Himpapawid ng Pilipinas (Philippines Air Force), Basa Airbase, Philippines, 1960.
First created in 1953 flying the P-51 Mustang, the team flew Sabres from 1958 until 1968.

BLUE DIAMONDS, PHILIPPINE AIR FORCE

From its founding in 1952 through to entering a period of indefinite hiatus in 2005, Blue Diamonds was the official aerobatic team of the Philippine Air Force.

At the beginning, two pilots flying P-51D Mustangs based at César Basa airbase gave brief performances. This was enough to convince their commander to establish a four-man team, participating in an airshow during Philippine Aviation Week in November 1953.

They received the name 'Blue Diamond' in 1954 in recognition of their classic diamond formation – though their aircraft were left in natural metal with the 'blue' apparently being a reference to the air force's signature colour.

The team was then expanded to five aircraft before the PAF's Mustangs were phased out in favour of T-33 jet trainers and Blue Diamond were temporarily disbanded. By 1957, the PAF had acquired F-86F Sabres and some Blue Diamond members were among those trained to fly them. As a result, the team re-formed with the new aircraft.

In 1958, Blue Diamond were expanded to eight aircraft and these were fitted with smoke generators – with a ninth machine being added in 1959. The name was also changed slightly at this point to become 'Blue Diamonds' plural.

The Blue Diamonds were flying up to 12 Sabres by 1961 and using coloured smoke, rather than the original white, but the following year their number was reduced back to nine with two reserves. The PAF began operating the Northrop F-5A Freedom Fighter in 1965 and the Blue Diamonds adopted this as their new mount in 1968, starting out with a six-man formation. This was reduced to four during the tough economic conditions of the mid-1970s before the team were disbanded for a second time in 1978. The economic crisis had abated by 1986 and the team then re-formed, returning to full strength with six F-5As. The team continued to fly until 2005 when they were disbanded for a third and perhaps final time due to the retirement of the PAF's Freedom Fighters.

GOLDEN SABRES, PHILIPPINE AIR FORCE

Two additional aerobatic teams were formed from the PAF, alongside the Blue Diamonds, in 1971: the Red Aces and the Golden Sabres, both flying F-86s. The latter were part of the 9th Tactical Fighter Squadron and made their show debut in early 1972 at Iba, Zambales.

The following year, however, the Golden Sabres found themselves short of pilots and were merged with the Red Aces to form a combined team named 'Sabres'. This lasted two more years before being disbanded.

MODERN AEROBATIC TEAMS **119**

MODERN AEROBATIC TEAMS
CHAPTER 5 – ASIA

SAUDI ARABIA

▼ BAE HAWK MK.65
BAe Hawk MK.65, Saudi Falcons, 8817, No. 88 Squadron, Royal Saudi Air Force, King Faisal Airbase, Tabuk Saudi Arabia, 2019.
The team was created in 1998 and has flown the Hawk since then; this year it was presented with the newest variant, the Hawk Mk.165.

SINGAPORE

▼ LOCKHEED-MARTIN F-16C FIGHTING FALCON
Lockheed-Martin F-16C Fighting Falcon, 5, Black Knights demonstration team, Republic of Singapore Air Force, Tengah airbase, Singapore, 2016.
The Black Knights operated F-16s sporadically from 2000-2015, first the F-16A and then the F-16C.

SAUDI FALCONS, ROYAL SAUDI AIR FORCE

The Saudi Falcons were created from No. 88 Squadron, based at King Abdulaziz airbase, on June 6, 1998. They fly six BAE Hawk Mk.65As plus three Mk.65s, all smoke-capable and painted in green and white, and are the Royal Saudi Air Force's official demonstration team. Their debut performance took place in January 1999 over Riyadh as part of Saudi Arabia's 100th anniversary celebrations. The Falcons' first international show followed in February 2000 when they appear in Bahrain and their first show in Europe took place in 2011 at Zeltweg, Austria.

The team received their first Hawk Mk.165 in February 2024, this being the RSAF's variant of the Hawk AJT – an upgrade to existing airframes that consists of modern LCD instrumentation and the Rolls-Royce Adour 951 engine. The latter is a fundamental redesign of the Adour Mk.106 with significantly improved performance and double the service life.

BLACK KNIGHTS, REPUBLIC OF SINGAPORE AIR FORCE

Starting out as 'Osprey Red' in 1973, flying four Hawker Hunters, the Singapore Air Force team was renamed Black Knights in 1974 – with 'black knight' being derived from the famously manoeuvrable chess piece.

The team then switched to flying five F-5E Tiger IIs in 1981 and then six A-4U Super Skyhawks in 1990. The team briefly operated as four Skyhawks and two F-16As in 2000 before entering an eight-year hiatus. They briefly returned with six F-16Cs to commemorate the 40th anniversary of the Republic of Singapore Air Force before returning to a dormant state for another six years. The team came back again for the Singapore Air Show in 2014 with a new paint scheme featuring the crescent moon and five stars of the national flag and the following year Black Knights 5 and 6 performed at the Avalon Air Show, with another Black Knights liveried F-16 on static display. A full team performance then took place as part of Singapore's Golden Jubilee celebrations that August. This was their last performance to date and the team appears to have since been dissolved with no plans to revive it.

MODERN AEROBATIC TEAMS **121**

MODERN AEROBATIC TEAMS CHAPTER 5 – ASIA

SOUTH KOREA

▼ NORTH AMERICAN F-86 SABRE
North American F-86 Sabre, 24777, Blue Sabres, Republic of Korea Air Force, South Korea, 1965. The Blue Sabres flew from 1962 until 1967.

▼ KAI T-50
KAI T-50, 8, Black Eagles, 239th Special Flying Squadron, Republic of Korea Air Force, Wonju airbase, South Korea, 2022. The RoKAF has operated several display teams since the end of the Korean War; the current one uses eight examples of the indigenous KAI T-50 trainer.

122 MODERN AEROBATIC TEAMS

BLUE SABRE, REPUBLIC OF KOREA AIR FORCE

The first aerobatic team of the Republic of Korea Air Force (RoKAF) was established in 1953 flying F-51 Mustangs and in October 1956 another team, the T-33A Show Flight Team, was formed. Their successor, established in October 1959, was the Blue Sabre team flying four specially painted F-86s. The aircraft colour scheme was changed several times up to 1967 when the team was disbanded.

BLACK EAGLES, REPUBLIC OF KOREA AIR FORCE

With the introduction of the F-5A Freedom Fighter, a new RcKAF display team was formed in 1967: the Black Eagles. They flew a formation of seven aircraft for three years before aerobatic training was suspended in 1970. The team recommenced their performances in 1973, now flying RF-5As. Five years later, the team was fully disbanded as the RoKAF concentrated on military preparedness.

The Black Eagles name languished in obscurity for the next 16 years before being revived and applied to a new team formed from the second flight of the 238th Fighter Squadron, 8th Fighter Wing, on December 12, 1994. Flying six Cessna A-37B Dragonflies, the team was detached from the 238th on April 1, 1999, and became the 239th Aerobatic Flight Squadron.

The team continued to fly their A-37Bs until 2007 when they were disbanded temporarily while transitioning to the new locally-made KAI T-50 Golden Eagle jet trainer. Their debut performance in this machine took place over Seoul on September 23, 2009, and commemorated the RoKAF's 60th anniversary.

Today the eight Black Eagles' T-50Bs are painted yellow, white and black and are fitted with internal smoke generators. They are stationed at Wonju airbase.

▼ CESSNA A-37B DRAGONFLY

Cessna A-37B Dragonfly, 794/1, Black Eagles, Republic of Korea Air Force, Wonju airbase, South Korea, 1996.
After roughly a decade of flying F-5s, the team was disbanded in the late 1970s; it would be re-established in 1994 flying the A-37.

MODERN AEROBATIC TEAMS

MODERN AEROBATIC TEAMS — CHAPTER 5 – ASIA

TAIWAN

▼ AIDC AT-3 TZU CHUNG
AIDC AT-3 Tzu Chung, AT-30849/77-6049, Thunder Tigers, Air Force Academy, Republic of China Air Force, Kangshan airbase, Taiwan, 2016.
The Thunder Tigers previously flew the F-84, the F-86 and later the F-5 aircraft; more recently they began using the indigenous AT-3.

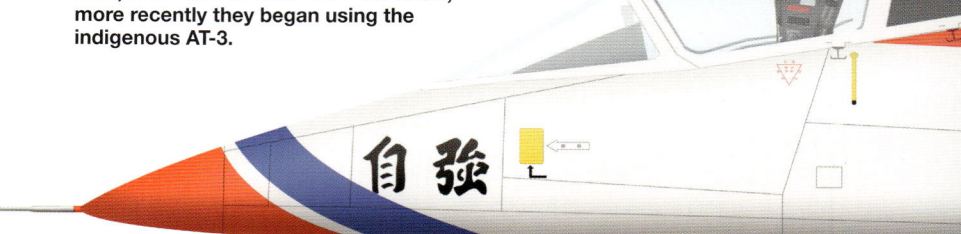

THAILAND

▼ PILATUS PC-9
Pilatus PC-9, 02, Blue Phoenix, 2nd Training Squadron, Flying Training School, Royal Thai Air Force, Nakhon Pathom airbase, Thailand, 2012.
In 2012, to celebrate the 100th anniversary of Aviation in Thailand, a new display team was set up within the 2nd TS.

UNITED ARAB EMIRATES

FURSAN AL EMARAT, UNITED ARAB EMIRATES AIR FORCE
Flying seven Aermacchi MB-339NAT jet trainers, Fursan Al Emarat or 'The Knights of the Emirates' is the aerobatic display team of the United Arab Emirates Air Force. The seven aircraft represent the seven Emirates.

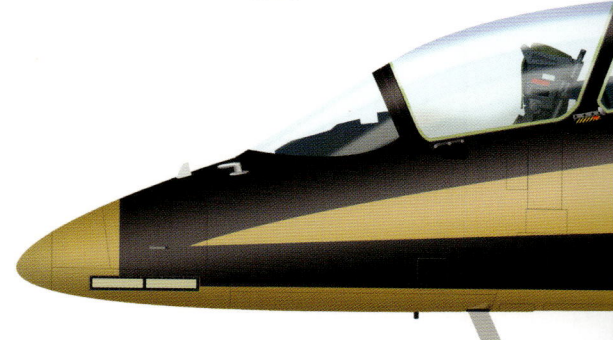

THUNDER TIGERS, REPUBLIC OF CHINA AIR FORCE

The Republic of China Air Force Thunder Tigers Aerobatics Team were founded in 1953 at Tainan airbase flying four F-84G Thunderjets. By 1957 the team had expanded to nine aircraft and their international debut took place during the Philippines International Air Show at Manila Airport on December 15 that year. Two years later, the team transitioned to the F-86 – known as the 'Dagger' in Taiwanese service.

The Daggers were swapped for F-5A Freedom Fighters in 1967 and these in turn gave way to F-5Es in 1975. Thirteen years later, in 1988, the team converted to nine locally-made AIDC AT-3 Tzu Chung jet trainers. These were painted in white, blue and red as well as being fitted with smoke generators.

The Thunder Tigers continue to perform today.

BLUE PHOENIX, ROYAL THAI AIR FORCE

Celebrations to mark the 100th anniversary of Thai aviation in 2012 included the formation of the first official Royal Thai Air Force aerobatic team: Blue Phoenix. They were equipped with five blue, white and red painted Pilatus PC-9 aircraft, each fitted with a white smoke generator.

Based at Nakhon Pathom's Kamphaeng Saen airbase, the team is part of the RTAF's Flying Training School squadron and all of its pilots are instructors.

The team usually perform at special events locally but have performed internationally too, including at RIAT in the UK.

▼ AERMACCHI MB-339NAT

Aermacchi MB-339NAT, 7, Fursan Al Emarat (Knights of the Emirates), Air Academy, United Arab Emirates Air Force, Al Ain airbase, UAE, 2012. The team fly seven aircraft representing the seven Emirates of the UAE.

MODERN AEROBATIC TEAMS

MODERN AEROBATIC TEAMS — CHAPTER 6 – OCEANIA

CHAPTER 6 – OCEANIA

AUSTRALIA

▼ CAC SABRE
CAC Sabre, A94-901, Black Panthers, 76 Squadron, Royal Australian Air Force, Williamtown airbase, Australia, 1965.
76 Squadron formed an aerobatic team (the Black Panthers) in 1965, flying the CAC Sabre.

▼ DASSAULT-GAF MIRAGE IIIO
Dassault-GAF Mirage IIIO, A3-19, Deltas, Royal Australian Air Force, Williamtown airbase, Australia, 1971.
The Deltas flew in standard camouflaged Mirages, drawn from several RAAF squadrons; this aircraft is from 77 Squadron.

▼ PILATUS PC-21
Pilatus PC-21, A54-033, Roulettes, Central Flying School, Royal Australian Air Force, East Sale airbase, Australia, 2020.
The current RAAF display team have flown the PC-21 since 2019.

CAC SABRE

CAC Sabre, A94-352, Black Diamonds, 75 Squadron, Royal Australian Air Force, Williamtown airbase, Australia, 1963.
The team consisted of four aircraft from 75 Squadron and performed from 1961-1964

BLACK DIAMONDS, ROYAL AUSTRALIAN AIR FORCE

Formed from 75 Squadron of the RAAF in 1961, the Black Diamonds flew four Commonwealth Aircraft Corporation CA-27 Mk.32 Sabres. Their paint scheme was bare metal with smart black highlights including a diamond on their forward fuselage sides and a top hat logo on their tails.
They disbanded just three years later when the squadron began transitioning to the Dassault Mirage III fighter.

BLACK PANTHERS, ROYAL AUSTRALIAN AIR FORCE

Like the Black Diamonds, the Black Panthers were equipped with four CAC CA-27 Sabres. Stationed at Williamtown airbase, they were drawn from 76 Squadron and performed from early 1965 to 1966. Their livery was similar to that of the Black Diamonds but with a large black panther on the forward fuselage and a mostly red fin.

DELTAS, ROYAL AUSTRALIAN AIR FORCE

It comes as little surprise to learn that the Deltas derived their name from the shape of their aircraft: the Mirage III. All were equipped with white smoke generators but wore only their standard in-service colours.
The Williamtown-based team flew seven aircraft – five for the main formation and two solos – and performed for the RAAF's 50th anniversary in 1971. They disbanded shortly thereafter.

ROULETTES, ROYAL AUSTRALIAN AIR FORCE

The Australian Central Flying School in Victoria established its own aerobatic team in 1962, known as the Red Sails. They flew de Havilland Vampire Mk.35 jet trainers but suffered a catastrophic loss on August 15, 1962, when six people were killed and four aircraft were lost. Their successors were the Telstars, formed in February 1963, still flying Vampires. They then received Macchi MB-326Hs in February 1968 but were disbanded after just two months to save money.
Two years later, the Central Flying School team was reconstituted with the MB-326s as the Roulettes to help celebrate the RAAF's 50th anniversary – their first show taking place at Point Cook in December 1970. The team continued to use the Macchis until 1989 when they switched to Pilatus PC-9s. They flew then six of these, plus a spare, for the next 30 years, up to 2019.
The PC-9s were then swapped for PC-21s – the RAAF's new trainer.
The aircraft are painted red with a white and blue pattern on top plus a big letter 'R' on the tail. Six of the seven Roulettes pilots are instructors, with the seventh serving as commentator and as ferry pilot for the spare aircraft.

MODERN AEROBATIC TEAMS

MODERN AEROBATIC TEAMS — CHAPTER 6 – OCEANIA

NEW ZEALAND

▼ NORTH AMERICAN HARVARD MK.II

North American Harvard MK.II, NZ1076, Red Checkers, Central Flying School, Royal New Zealand Air Force, Ohakea airbase, New Zealand, 1975.
The team initially flew Harvards before switching to the CT/4 during their final years.

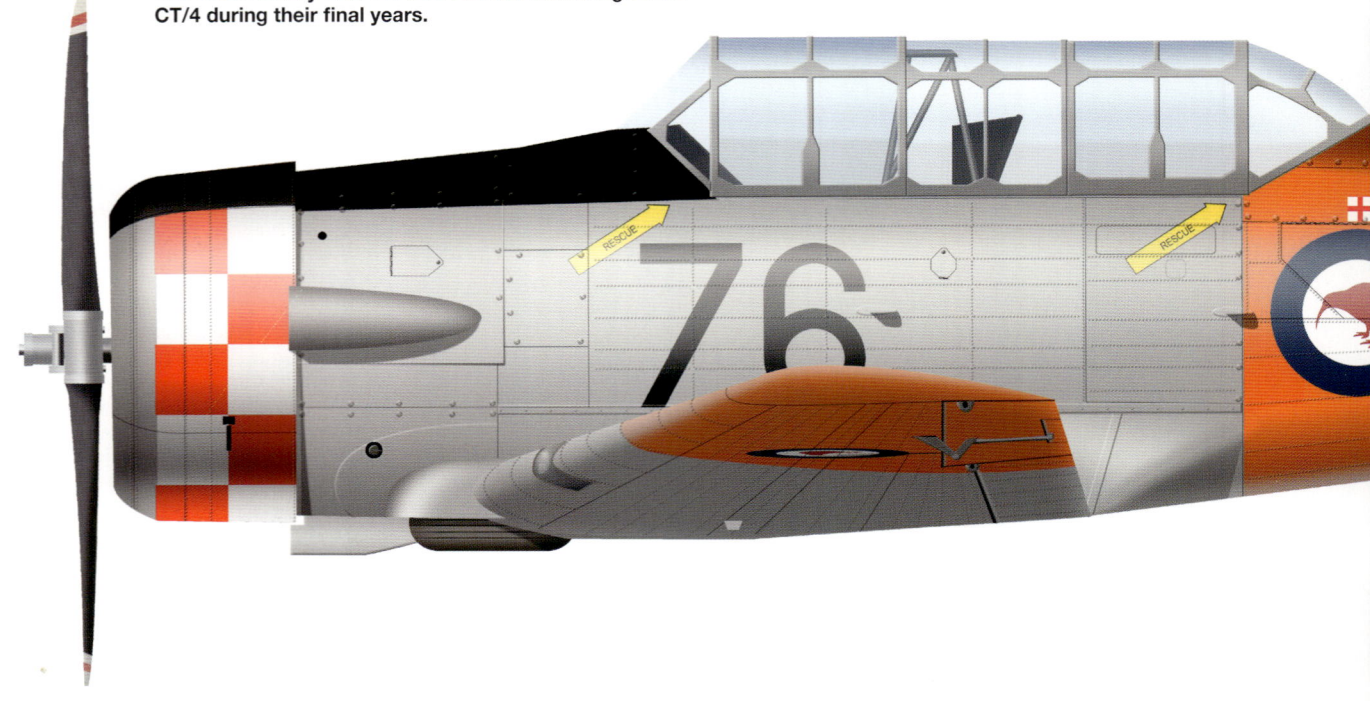

▼ BEECHCRAFT T-6 TEXAN II

Beechcraft T-6 Texan II, NZ1410, Black Falcons, Central Flying School, Royal New Zealand Air Force, Ohakea airbase, New Zealand, 2017.
Having briefly flown MB-339s, the current Black Falcons fly T-6s.

RED CHECKERS, ROYAL NEW ZEALAND AIR FORCE

The Red Checkers were the aerobatic display team of the Royal New Zealand Air Force between 1967 and 2014. Formed from the RNZAF Central Flying School, they were equipped with five Harvard trainers. Then, in 1973, they were temporarily disbanded due to the global fuel crisis. After a seven-year hiatus, they returned in 1980 flying four locally-made Pacific Aerospace Corporation CT/4B Airtrainers.

They continued to fly displays until 2014 when they were disbanded with the retirement of the CT/4s.

BLACK FALCONS, ROYAL NEW ZEALAND AIR FORCE

Originally formed in 2000 and composed of instructors, the team flew five Aermacchi MB-339CB jet trainers from 14 Squadron. They appeared for just five displays, starting on January 1, 2000, and were then disbanded.

With the Red Checkers having been dissolved in 2014, and with the Central Flying School now using Beechcraft T-6 Texan IIs, it was decided that the Black Falcons name should be revived and applied to a new team equipped with seven of those aircraft.

The revived Black Falcons is still made up of flying instructors, with the team leader, Falcon 1, usually being the Officer Commanding Central Flying School. Currently, the Black Falcons fly around 150 shows annually.

Mortons Books

Messerschmitt Me 262: Development & Politics

by Dan Sharp

There are many myths surrounding the development of the Messerschmitt Me 262 jet fighter. Its unparalleled performance is beyond doubt; easily able to outpace its opponents and possessing the firepower to shred them in seconds. Yet immediately after the Second World War, rumours abounded that official indifference, technical shortcomings, and interference from the Führer himself had crippled the Me 262's progress and delayed its appearance on the front line until it was far too late.

Begun as a series of design concepts during 1938, the fighter would not enter mass production until the spring of 1944. Even then it failed to make any notable impact until the closing weeks of the war, when Me 262s began destroying USAAF bombers at an alarming rate. Exactly what happened to cause this apparently late start and who was responsible has until now been largely a matter of conjecture.

Grounded in research involving thousands of wartime documents spread across archival collections in three countries, Messerschmitt Me 262 Development & Politics finally sweeps aside the myths and provides a clear understanding of the real history. Sharp examines the aircraft's technical development in unparalleled detail as well as analysing the ongoing discussions surrounding the Me 262 at the highest levels within the Messerschmitt company, the German Air Ministry and Adolf Hitler's inner circle.

ONLY £30

"No matter how many of those previous Me 262 titles you own, this one deserves to accompany them. It's a fine authorial achievement."
- Aeroplane magazine, Book of the Month January 2023

ORDER NOW: www.mortonsbooks.co.uk Or call 01507 529529

WANT TO HEAR ABOUT OUR LATEST BOOKS?

Mortons Books publishes a selection of high-quality titles by authors who are true experts in their field. For the best reads on railway, military and aviation history to consumer issues, hobbies, crime, and politics, look no further.

If you would like to hear more about our upcoming book releases and special offers, sign up to our newsletter.